Confessions of a Highland Hero

Confessions of a Highland Hero

STEVE 'PELE' PATERSON

WITH FRANK GILFEATHER

BIRLINN

For my mother, Margaret, daughters Jessica and Emily,
and all my family and close friends

This edition first published in 2010 by
Birlinn Limited
West Newington House
10 Newington Road
Edinburgh
EH9 1QS

www.birlinn.co.uk

ISBN: 978 1 84158 916 9

British Library Cataloguing-in-Publication Data
A catalogue record for this book is available from the British Library

Typeset by Iolaire Typesetting, Newtonmore
Printed and bound by JF Print Ltd, Somerset

Contents

List of Illustrations

Happy families in Mosstodloch.

The Manchester United first-team squad, 1979–80.

The hairstyle that prompted the nickname 'Big Bird'.

From Mosstodloch to Manchester and early commercial opportunities by the club's marketing people.

A collectors' item at Old Trafford.

In action for Tokyo in the mid-1980s.

Early success at Elgin City with my assistant Mike Winton.

Happy days at Huntly where we carried all before us. *Huntly Express*

Celebrating our second Highland League championship win. *Huntly Express*

The Caley Thistle squad, 1998–99. *Trevor Martin*

Steve Lennox and I show off the Qualifying Cup, the league championship trophy and the Aberdeenshire Cup in 1995. *Huntly Express*

With St Johnstone's Paul Sturrock as we are congratulated by Sir Alex Ferguson. *SNS Pix*

Former Home Secretary Dr John Reid poses for pictures with Doug McGilivray and me at the Caledonian Stadium. *Trevor Martin*

Mandy with our daughters Emily and Jessica in December 1996. *Aberdeen Journals Limited*

Foreword

Sportsmen and women are human beings, and as human beings they are prone to human conditions. At Sporting Chance the conditions we primarily deal with are addictions, the manifestations of which can be depression, anxiety and stress.

Of course many people's perception of addiction is coloured by the fact that they have never experienced it themselves, and they often define it in moral terms – a lack of character, weakness and selfish indulgence. When the sufferer is a public figure, a 'Highland hero' who has enjoyed the trappings of an illustrious career, the belief that the talents have been squandered through choice is also held by many. But addiction does not preclude anyone and does not differentiate in terms of fame or wealth. Addiction unaddressed devastates careers and families, and the paradox is that the illness tells you that you don't have a problem, but in order to recover from it you have to admit you do have a problem!

Steve Paterson has my admiration for facing his demons, as do all those who seek help through Sporting Chance. From the founding trustee, Tony Adams, to my core clinical team, we have all been in the position where addiction has taken over our lives and wreaked havoc for us and those close to us. Steve sought help and embarked on our programme with the same grit, determination and fortitude that made him the player and coach that he was. The programme is tough and requires an individual to confront his or her behaviour, with all its ramifications, breaking down the barriers that have up till then prevented them from acknowledging their problem. Wallowing in self pity does not address the issue. As we say, 'Poor me, poor me, pour me a drink.' Steve stopped the 'poor me's' and focused on the solutions.

It is not an easy road to recovery, even at a centre such as ours, and it takes determination and discipline to win through. Some people have periods of relapse, but the fighters, of which Steve is one, pick themselves up again and carry on. Rarely have we seen a person fail who has followed our path.

Steve, we hope you will continue your walk down that path.

Peter Kay
Chief Executive Officer
The Sporting Chance Clinic
September 2009

No sporting certainty

The tranquillity of Hampshire was welcoming as I arrived at Forest Mere, 160 acres of sublime and natural beauty where I convinced myself that this broken man could be fixed.

'Good luck, mate.' The taxi driver, who had driven me from the railway station in the nearby village of Liphook on a chilly, late-September Sunday evening in 2008, broke his silence as I stepped from his cab and looked at the magnificent mansion before me.

Did my appearance really indicate to the cabbie that I was a gambling addict with a serious drink problem? Was that why he voiced his friendly message? Why hadn't he assumed that I was simply a guest at Champneys, the plush hotel and spa I was about to enter? After all, the Sporting Chance Clinic occupies two buildings 400 metres behind the mansion and is hidden by woods. Maybe I had that 'haunted' look of a man struggling with his demons. Or was this paranoia kicking-in?

I was nervous and a touch apprehensive as I pushed open the front door and the receptionist greeted me.

'Are you here for Sporting Chance?' She, too, could tell my predicament, I thought. Her smile and the warmth in her voice, however, were genuine, and in an instant I felt at ease.

This is it, I thought. It was no sporting certainty but an opportunity, a lifeline that just a couple of weeks earlier I never dreamt would be available to me. Could I really find a way out of my living hell? Might I dare hope that the years of gambling and drinking, of lies, deceit and even theft, could now be about to be consigned to history?

'Thank you, God, for offering me your help', a little voice whispered inside my head.

What would I have done without the financial assistance of the Professional Footballers' Association, who provided the funding for the rehabilitation programme on which I was about to embark? Where would I be today had I not had true friends and my lovely daughters and my mother who never gave up hope of my salvation? All these thoughts raced through my mind as I was led to my room for the night.

The following morning I reported to the main house of the clinic within the Forest Mere grounds, quiet and secluded and away from the luxurious main complex. As part of the Sporting Chance Clinic's tailor-made programmes, I was told, clients – that is how patients like me are described – were free to use Champneys gym, swimming pool, sauna and steam room as well as its various alternative therapies. Oh yes, and we would be eating at the superb award-winning restaurant where the food was in accordance with the nutritional ethos laid down by the clinic. The Sporting Chance concept, it was stressed, was all about an holistic approach for the mind, the body and the spirit.

For the first time in years of despair and depression I felt comfortable with myself, helped by the commonality I shared with fellow clients and remembering how Tony Adams, a first-rate centre half with Arsenal and England, had conquered his alcoholism and founded this wonderful facility, which was to be home for just over four weeks.

The clinic opened its doors in 2000 but didn't start working with patients until two years later. Soon, it evolved into one of the most innovative centres of its kind, dealing with the treatment of the behavioural problems of professional sports people.

'How lucky am I?' I kept repeating to myself.

Peter Kay, the clinic's chief executive, shares Adams's thinking, and he leads the team of professionals put in place to facilitate the needs of those, like me, who have dropped off the edge of normality.

In the days leading up to this moment I had read as much as I could about Sporting Chance, but a line or two on its website struck me more than anything else. The words belonged to Adams: 'I wish Peter and the team had been around when I was wrestling with my demons. That's why I would say to any professional sportsman or woman out there trying to get through without guidance; on your own you've got no chance. With Peter and the team you've got a great chance – a Sporting Chance.'

Here I was, set to embark on a journey into the unknown but content to place myself in the capable and experienced hands of a group of strangers whose knowledge of me was restricted to a meeting six weeks earlier when I was assessed by them to ascertain whether I was ready to surrender myself to their expertise. At that time, they knew little about me but they would soon learn the depth of my myriad difficulties.

Was I ready to pour out my heart about the sums of money – totalling a conservative £1.3 million – I had gambled away over a period of 34 years? Could I bring myself to open up about the drinking that led to the break-up of my marriage and another close relationship, and what all that did to my daughters? How would they react to my stories of stealing from my elderly mother? What would they think at Forest Mere when I told them about my mad world?

I was to learn, of course, that such tales of distress and desperation were commonplace inside that special haven. They were the stories of all addicts. All I was required to do was to hand myself over to them and trust that everything they could offer me would be beneficial.

With my induction over and a run-down of counselling and classes laid out before me, I was ready.

I lay in my bed that first night and prayed to God for

guidance. I thanked him, too, for bringing this opportunity to a wee boy from the Highlands of Scotland who had lost his way in life, a lost soul at the head of a trail of human and emotional debris.

Looking around the immediate vicinity of the clinic brought to mind my idyllic childhood in rural Moray in the north-east of Scotland, a habitat that incorporated the River Spey, its surrounding woods and fields, the picturesque and historic village of Garmouth and, just slightly to the north, the Moray Firth.

I was born in Mosstodloch, a nondescript community nestling a mile or so from Fochabers, the home of the world-renowned Baxters food complex, a cottage industry which grew to become one of the most famous of Scottish brands.

The third of four children, I entered the world on 8 April 1958 in the council house of my parents, Margaret and Bill. My father was an intelligent yet distant man who had studied Latin and English at school, went to university in Aberdeen, but dropped out and became a telephone engineer with the old GPO, with whom he spent his entire working life of 46 years.

My mother had been born into a Quaker family in the fishing port of Grimsby and, along with her two sisters and her brother, was evacuated to Bogmoor, not far from Mosstodloch, to the east of the Spey, when German bombers struck her home town in 1940.

She never left Moray and she and my father married there in 1949, moving into one of the dozen council houses then in Mosstodloch and settling into what was then a traditional family way of life, where the man of the house worked and the woman remained at home to cook, clean and look after the children.

Apart from lighting the coal fire, my father did nothing around the house and my mother was largely his, and our, servant – although she did not see it that way.

My brother, Neil, was seven years older than me while

Morag, my sister, was five years my senior. Andy, the baby of the family, came along five years after I was born, so our house was not only pretty cramped but it was noisy and busy most of the time.

Perhaps that's why I enjoyed the outdoors so much; the open fields, the wooded areas around the Spey, one of the great salmon rivers of the world, and the local park, where I seemed to spend most of my days playing football.

Memories often trick minds into believing every day of a childhood was sunny and perfect. That's how I remember it as I grew up. But then my part of the world is famous for its softer climes, created by the warm gulfstream which comes into the Moray Firth and bathes much of the area and makes it a favourite destination for photographers for its dramatic and diverse coastline.

Mosstodloch and the surrounding vicinity had everything I ever wanted and, no matter where in the world I have hung my hat, I have been drawn back to a community I am proud to call home. I am a village lad, a country boy at heart.

My love affair with football started at an early age. My mother has told me numerous times that I spent more time playing the game than I ever did in the house. That is because, during the 1966 World Cup in England, I became infatuated with the man born Edson Arantes Do Nascimento: known simply as Pele. I was eight years old and along with all the other boys in the village, I was hooked on the black and white BBC television coverage of the tournament won by England.

We were glued to games involving Franz Beckenbauer and Uve Seeler of Germany, or West Germany as they were known before the demolition of the Berlin Wall; Bobby Moore and Bobby Charlton of England; and Garrincha and Jairzinho of Brazil. For me, though, there was only one player I ever wanted to be: Pele. When my group of pals gathered for our daily game of football, even if there was only two of us, I was Pele. I might be Steve Paterson outwith my own neck of the woods, but in the north of Scotland I am still known as Pele.

Bill, my father, was largely uninterested in anything outside his work, certainly not in my participation in structured football, either with the local boys' club in Elgin or in the Sunday team for which I played under a man called Jimmy Shanks. Shanks was a diehard football fanatic and anybody and everybody from a wide radius of Fochabers whom he considered good enough would be drafted in to play for one of his teams, known as 'Shankies'.

He was a local plumber and scouted for Cardiff City, then managed by a Scot, Jimmy Scoular. Shanks had discovered Don Murray, a young lad from Duffus, near where I lived, who became one of Cardiff's longest-serving players and on the back of this success, many youngsters from Moray, including me, were to spend their Easter or summer holidays on trial with the Welsh club.

Jimmy Shanks was a great character who loved football and spent much of his time trawling the local villages in his beat-up Bedford van and wearing his overalls, gathering his team for the forthcoming match on a Sunday. You always knew he was approaching your house. 'One sugar and a spot of milk, please; no biscuits.' Those words were his calling card. As he had probably been to several houses before mine, he was always able to give me a rundown on who was playing in the team that weekend.

Playing for Shankies and being transported to away games sitting among plumbers' tools and spare tyres in the back of the Bedford and hoping for a trial at Cardiff City was all part of life for local lads around Fochabers during the late 1960s and early '70s.

We would compete against teams from other coastal towns and I was with him from an early age, right through until I was 16. From the age of 15 I would play for my school – Milne's

High School, Fochabers – on Saturday mornings, then for a junior side in the afternoon and for Jimmy's team on Sundays. I thought nothing of it, although my knees are paying for it now.

From the age of 10 I became involved in organised league football through Elgin Boys' Club which ran a number of teams through different age groups. You were allocated a team after you enrolled during the Easter holidays. The club was founded in 1964 by a local lawyer called John Cameron, an early influence on me and my football. John used to coach the local boys' select, of which I was captain, and we would occasionally travel abroad to compete in tournaments. Cameron introduced systems and tactics unheard of at the time and was a keen student of football technique.

Later, while still at Milne's High School, I played for Nairn County in the Highland League on Saturdays and Jimmy Shanks's team on Sundays. I was a naturally two-footed player, which was unusual among young boys, and I displayed that aptitude by taking free kicks and penalties with either foot. This ability, allied to whatever other in-built talent I possessed, made me better than my peers and brought me to the attention of several clubs in the Highland League, where on-field personnel were uncompromising and teams were made up of mature men with a win-at-any-cost mentality.

Perhaps my obsession with football blinkered me to my father's battle with depression. In those days mental illness carried a stigma which meant it was never discussed, not even within the family, and while I was close to my mother and that never changed, I had never appreciated or understood my dad's suffering.

All I knew was that he was a sad and lonely man who had difficulty relating to his children. Could that have been because, as an only child, he was raised by his mother, a headmistress in a rural school in Kellas, after she and my grandfather had divorced?

Divorce was another subject which, at the time, would have

been swept under the carpet and never spoken of. It was heartbreaking that, although his father lived not far away, in Forres, my dad had had no contact with him after the break-up of the marriage. I never really knew my grandmother, as she died in 1965 when I was just seven years old.

My father worked hard all his life but he rarely enjoyed himself and never had a holiday, and right up until the time I left home, aged 17, he had never demonstrated any interest in football or how well I was doing in the sport – although strangely my managerial career later in my life enthused him.

The absence of affection from him, however, didn't register with me or my siblings. After all, working-class families rarely displayed any kind of emotion and my dad's sadness and quiet nature were just part of the scene at 10 Garmouth Road, our three-bedroom local authority abode.

It was there that he would frequently leave the living room and go off on his own into the kitchen where he would sit slumped at the table for hours on end, staring into space.

He never addressed his depression until later in his life, when he consulted a doctor after years of suffering in silence. His spirits were lifted for a couple of years when he was given medication which made him a much happier and more content person. Once he came off his anti-depressants, though, he sank once more. My father died of pancreatic cancer in 2001. He was 73 years old.

I attended a small rural primary school called Balnacoul in 1963. There were only about half a dozen other pupils in my class and from the age of five I loved joining in with the older boys playing football at break times.

The entire school roll would have barely reached 50. So, once the girls embarked on their skipping or hopscotch or other playground games, it was jerseys off for goalposts for the boys, playing anything from eight-a-side to fifteen-a-side.

One incident from Primary 1 which my sister Morag refuses

to let me forget, proved rather embarrassing and marked me down from an early age as a poor liar. I had an issue about using the school toilets and would certainly never do my 'main business' there. So, I would try to hold on until I reached the security and familiarity of my home.

One day, I failed miserably and was forced to squat at the side of the road, about half a mile from my house. For whatever reason, instead of fleeing the scene, I hung around until the older kids, including Morag, came out of school. I stood beside the human waste and pointed out that a dog 'had made a mess'.

This ridiculous claim was met with uproarious laughter by the older group who knew a dog turd when they saw one. I was exposed to public humiliation which, at the age of five, I found too much to bear. I ran home crying and took a long time to live down that embarrassing incident.

A couple of years later I was at the centre of a generous act – a good old-fashioned display of Christianity – that put me in a better light. There were a few poor families in the area whose children attended Balnacoul and the clothing of some was ragged and inadequate, especially for the harsh Highland winters.

A wee boy from a family of travellers lived in an old caravan about half a mile from the village. His old plimsolls were torn and shredded, he wore a flimsy jumper and he would cry with the cold while plodding his way home. I always felt pity for him and would give him my duffle coat to keep him warm and I would lift him on to my back and give him a 'piggy' home. I was a big lad for my age and the proud owner of Wellington boots and was pleased to do my bit for this puny little lad. The family moved away by the summer.

I was still at primary school when I discovered Elgin City Football Club with their black and white vertical striped jerseys and their neat ground, Borough Briggs. On Saturdays I would often hitchhike from Mosstodloch into Moray's main town and savour the delights on offer on the pitch. I would be extra excited when a team from the Scottish Football League would visit for a cup-tie or, sometimes, for a friendly. It wasn't unusual in those days for several thousand fans to pack Borough Briggs to watch their favourites, players who were my heroes.

The 1960s was an especially successful period for the club and in 1968 there were victories over league opposition in the shape of Albion Rovers, Forfar and Arbroath in Scottish Cup-ties, the latter game being watched by 12,650 fans at Borough Briggs. You can imagine my joy, then, when the club invited me to train with them in 1973. I was just 15 years old, the youngest player to turn out for Elgin City and I scored a goal in a 6-1 rout of Buckie Thistle. What a day that was for a schoolboy footballer, to be able to play alongside men of whom I was in awe, stalwarts of the club like Gerry Graham and George Gilbert.

Willie Grant, who revelled in the moniker 'The King', had been my idol of those giant-killing games of the '60s. He was a fantastic header of the ball and a prolific scorer of that era who was later to become a great friend and mentor when I became a manager. He was a true gentleman and remarkably modest about being an Elgin City and Highland League legend.

The following season I played for Nairn County under coaches Innes McDonald and George Welsh. Innes was a physical education teacher at Elgin Academy while George was head of PE at Gordonstoun, the famous public school in Moray attended by several members of the royal family.

Innes and George's involvement in school football was influential in attracting young would-be stars of the future, who knew their game would be improved under their tutelage. Those men became my mentors in the season prior to my joining Manchester United.

2

Gambling: an introduction

It was just before my Elgin City baptism that I turned out for Bishopmill United, a junior club in the Moray town, where I had my first formal coaching and training. I was, of course, still at school. But while I was bright enough, I was always Mr 55 per cent. In short, I passed my exams, but only just. School, for me, was simply part of my social life, where I could indulge in my new-found hobbies: three-card brag and shoot pontoon for money, and under-age drinking. It was more Milne's Social Club than Milne's High School.

If my card school at Milne's allowed me to flirt with gambling, my first real, gripping and, as it turned out, miserable experience of gambling came at the annual agricultural show at Keith, a busy town eight miles to the south of Mosstodloch. The weekend show was a huge attraction in those days and I was drawn to it as a youngster because it was atmospheric and fun. And it had penny arcades with one-arm bandits.

The first time I attended the show, in August 1970 when I was about 12, I was armed with plenty of pocket money as my gang of friends and I set off in the morning to savour anything the event could offer.

We had worked all week picking berries at the fields owned by Baxters and had plenty of cash in our pockets as we caught the Aberdeen-bound bus to head for the action. Those penny arcades and one-arm bandits certainly pulled me in and I found it extremely difficult to walk away from them.

Pretty soon I had lost everything, including the bus fare back to Mosstodloch which should have been set aside, like my friends had done. But the buzz I felt at the arcades had me hooked and I was determined that the fun wasn't going to stop. The problem was that I needed more money.

I discovered one tent in the showground where young lads just a little older than me, went in with empty trays and came out a little later laden with small tubs of ice cream to sell. This fuelled my curiosity and so I asked the man in the tent what it was all about.

'You get a tray of 24 tubs,' he growled, 'and when you've sold them all, come back and I'll give you your commission . . . one shilling.'

I volunteered myself and my foray into ice cream sales worked well. 'Ice cream, ice cream. Get your ice cream', was the simplicity of my sales pitch. A couple of hours later I had shifted four trays of the stuff and earned my cut, which was more than enough for the bus fare home to Mosstodloch.

First, though, it was back to that magical land of the penny arcades where I was to be introduced to the demons that were to haunt me for the rest of my life. Even at this early age there were clear signs that my fascination with risking money on the outcome of chance was abnormal. Having already lost all my berry-picking money I couldn't resist losing the ice cream commission, despite the obvious consequences that would follow. I was out of control and, after my travel expenses had evaporated, I had to face a long and lonely walk home as my punishment. No lessons were learned, unfortunately. Rather, it was to be the theme for my future life as a gambling addict.

There were other money-making opportunities, of course, and when my friends and I weren't playing football, we would take on seasonal work which included berry-picking in the summer, potato-gathering in the autumn and at Easter-time we would pluck weeds at a local nursery, Christie's, where we would also bundle young trees into bunches of 52.

My mates and I were inseparable and I don't think there would be disagreement among them that I was the leader, the dominant figure, and if we weren't concentrating on our main focus – football – or working during the school vacations, we would be climbing trees, poaching for salmon with net and gaff in the Spey, or digging underground dens in the woods surrounding the river. Long spring and summer days, happy and healthy.

If I was showing signs of going off the rails, nobody noticed. At least, if they did, they never mentioned it to me and there was certainly no hint that my parents suspected anything untoward about my behaviour, not even when I was carried home from a friend's house at Hogmanay having drunk myself unconscious with whisky and strong export beer. I was 12 years old.

Then, there was a terrifying incident one winter's night in 1971 when a boy five years my senior tried to drown me in the River Spey. Even to this day, it sends shivers down my spine.

I was 13 years old and this young man, a local bully who always seemed to latch on to much younger boys he knew he could influence, coerced me into becoming his accomplice in a series of thefts of lead and copper and other metals for which he could gain good money from scrap merchants.

He was drawn to younger lads, probably because he felt superior in their company. I was impressed and terrified of him at the same time, yet looked up to him. Although I had just entered my teens, at 6ft tall I appeared much older. I was also fit and agile and able to help him remove lead from the roofs of disused buildings or copper piping from other premises.

We had been doing this for six months when late one crisp and cold January night, with the sky clear and the moon bright, he convinced me that he had stashed away some of the stolen gear under a rock in the river.

By the light only of the moon, he led me half a mile through the woods to the river bank, where he waded in up to his thighs.

'Come on,' he beckoned. 'It's under this rock. You'll have to give me a hand.'

I entered the black, freezing water and gingerly shuffled my way next to him when he suddenly put me in a headlock and forced me under the water.

He was strong and powerful and held me firm as I writhed and wriggled under the surface of the fast-flowing river. I pushed and shoved and elbowed him trying to free myself, but each time I managed to come up for air, I was wrestled down again.

It was like something from a horror movie. I could hear him grunting as he did his best to hold my head still under the water. He was on his knees and was putting all the pressure he could muster on the headlock in which he held me.

At last, after what seemed like an eternity, with an enormous amount of energy that I found from somewhere and a determination that I wasn't going to die, I wriggled free. I scrambled my way to the embankment as he tried to grab me, shouting: 'I'll get you, you bastard.'

Once on dry land, I ran faster than I've ever done as my mind tried to take in that this crazy man had just tried to kill me. I knew only too well that he had not yet given up his quest to snuff out my life.

I was too quick for him and although he was in hot pursuit, I raced through the woods and on to the main road, the A96, over the Spey Bridge and ran for my life. Fear kept me running. I was overcome with a need to survive this horrific ordeal and once I was back on home turf and under the street lights of Mosstodloch, I slumped exhausted on to the pavement and sat dripping wet, shivering and hypothermic. I cried my eyes out knowing I couldn't tell anyone – not my family and certainly not the police – for fear of being locked up.

It was the most frightening experience of my life and I was left traumatised by my brush with death. Now it is an incident which remains largely locked away in my mind, resurfacing occasionally as I grow older. But still, it haunts me.

As for my would-be killer, I kept my distance from him. My gut instinct was that he had intended to drown me. This was no mere attempt to frighten me, of that I am sure. God knows what became of him. Did any other victim suffer from his warped mind? In any case, he left the village soon after and was never seen again.

3

The Bisto tin bank

At the age of 14 I started under-age drinking regularly, again with my usual crowd, and would be served without question in the Stag Bar in Elgin. It was a sleazy joint but we would never dream of moving pubs for fear that some other place would refuse us our pints of beer.

Our visits to the Stag became a ritual every weekend and later became part of the football culture where you would hit the pub after every game. I was once caught drinking in the Tower Bar, also in Elgin, where the Bishopmill United players would assemble to get drunk and dissect that day's match.

The police were cracking down on under-age drinking and one night, when I was just 15 years old, they raided the pub. Me and some of my friends escaped out of a toilet window and legged it, forgetting that I had, stupidly, left behind my club blazer and my holdall, items through which I was easily traced. I was hauled into the police station with my father and lectured about the ills of alcohol and told to stay away from pubs. It was water off a duck's back and I returned to my usual ways the following weekend. I saw it as a normal part of football life and, in any case, I liked alcohol and the feeling it gave me.

All my influences in life were outside the family home. My parents knew nothing of my misbehaviour or, indeed, any of the activities that went on when I shut the house door behind me. Home was for food and shelter. Had I lived in a city I have no doubt I would have been a member of a gang, because I was into exploration and experimentation.

A prime example of my wayward adolescence came in May 1973 when my mates and I made the long trek to Wembley for the Home Championship match between England and Scotland. It was a huge pilgrimage in those days, with thousands of Scots descending on London in tartan attire.

My 'magnificent seven' from Milne's High School had planned carefully for the adventure. We clubbed together and bought a battered old Transit van for £100 and we wondered at various stages of our journey whether we would make it to our destination.

Mike Hendry, one of my best school pals, had just passed his driving test and had the onerous task of getting us there safely and on time. An older lad from Fochabers, Roddy Munro, was a maths teacher in London and his flat was to be our base.

We set off from home at 6 a.m. on the eve of the big game, dressed in our kilts and Scotland jerseys, in a van packed with beer and lager. Needless to say, by the time we reached London we were all drunk – apart from Mike, of course – and we spent the evening with the hordes of Scotland supporters gathered in Trafalgar Square, singing and dancing in the fountain.

The game was a side-show – England won 1–0 with a Martin Peters goal – as the weekend evolved into a gigantic party. I enjoyed the atmosphere and the bright lights of London so much that, even though I was just 15 years old, I decided to extend my stay, another indication of my inability to withdraw from my pursuit of pleasure. Roddy, the teacher, was on holiday and did little to discourage me from staying on.

'Tell my mum and dad I'll be home next week,' I shouted to the departing desperados as I waved them on their way to Moray and I remained with Roddy, still a friend today and one who could be described as a bit of an eccentric. He had long, flowing locks and a colourful, some might say outlandish, dress sense, in the style of Billy Connolly.

He was a witty person who liked nothing better than to drive his Harley Davidson. I was to become his regular pillion passenger for the following week, a period spent, because I had no change of clothing, in my Tartan Army uniform.

For all my misdemeanours, I was still starring as the best young footballer in the area and, at the age of 16 – although I never knew it – I stood on the verge of joining one of the greatest football clubs in the world.

I was capped for the Scotland Schoolboys' under-18 side against England at Old Trafford, the home of Manchester United. It was the summer of 1974 and that game was to accelerate my progress from gifted youngster from the Highlands – who just might make the grade – to a talent with the potential to hit the high spots. Coming from a remote part of Scotland meant I wasn't on the radar of any professional clubs. They did not see such sparsely-populated areas as ones for rich pickings.

Yet, through the schools' system, I was propelled into the spotlight against the cream of England's young players all of whom would, like my own team-mates, be preparing to join the professional ranks the minute they left school.

I was a versatile performer, able to operate in most positions. I preferred a striking role but, at 6ft 2in tall and an imposing figure, I was selected to play at centre half. We drew 1-1 and, by general consensus, I was seen as the man-of-the-match.

The scouts of clubs throughout the land who were present that day sat up and took notice. They liked my confident attitude, my presence, that I possessed a high level of skill and that I could read the game well.

I hardly had time to return to Moray after the game when the Manchester United chief scout came knocking on my door to tell me he had seen enough to recognise that I had what was required to make it in the big time of English football and that Old Trafford wanted me.

I would not, the scout told me, be signed as an apprentice and all the boot cleaning and dressing room sweeping duties that went with that role. I would join as a full professional.

Tommy Docherty was the manager and he travelled to my home a short time later to seal the deal as I still tried to come to terms with the enormity of what the chief scout had earlier told me. Could it really be true that I was wanted by such a big football club and by the man who, prior to taking on the manager's job there, had been in charge of the Scotland international team? I was about to be propelled into the big time.

It was agreed that I would be allowed to remain in Moray to complete my schooling and to take my Higher examinations at Milne's High School the following year. I would, they instructed me, join United for pre-season training in the summer of 1975.

During one of the meetings between Manchester United's representatives, my parents and me, in my living room in Garmouth Road, the issue of the 'sweetener' was raised.

Without warning, one of the club's envoys took bundles of banknotes from his pockets, each bundle rolled up and held together by an elastic band, and placed them on the table around which we sat.

Few words, other than 'this is for you' to no one in particular, were uttered and my parents just stared, open-jawed, at the fortune in front of them.

Ten times the man from United went into his pockets and plucked one bundle after another, placing them on the table as we watched in silence.

My parents weren't worldly. They lived day by day, paid the rent and other bills and were, like many working-class couples, broke by the end of the week. They reacted to this pile of cash before them with disbelief. I swear there was fear in their eyes. They simply didn't know how to react. They never touched it, never spoke about it, never mentioned it in any future conversation. When the United delegation left, my parents ignored the money on the table as if it didn't exist and simply left it lying there. They wanted nothing to do with it. There was no thought or discussion about the possibility of banking it or setting up a trust fund for me for later in my life.

With the men from Man United gone, I counted the cash; ten wads each of £100, a total of £1000. In 2009 terms it is the equivalent of £12,500.

I knew then why my parents were apprehensive and be-mused. This was like winning the football pools and being bewildered and uncertain about what to do. But I certainly knew exactly what to do and I stuffed the £1000 into a brown Bisto tin and stored it at the bottom of my parents' wardrobe. For the following year, that tin was to be my personal bank and its contents my entry to a life which hitherto had been beyond me: gambling for much higher stakes.

The Bisto tin was a bit like an Aladdin's lamp for me. It would grant my wishes by delivering riches and I made sure it was used in the only way I knew how: to provide me with the best clothes I could get in the boutiques of Elgin, and for serious card games and big-money bets on the horses.

I was 16 years old and living the life of Riley. The book-maker's in Elgin, with its board markers and commentary via the Tannoy, became my world, a magical place that presented me with the kind of buzz I had never experienced.

Out of my half-dozen best pals – Mike Hendry, Jon Law, Doug Will, Franny Slater, Ainslie Gordon and Les Newlands – I was the one who had the real addiction. I loved gambling much more than any of the others. I pushed for and organised the regular card schools and was the one who thrived on the trips to the bookies.

I dipped into the Bisto tin bank constantly, whenever I needed money, and my parents were completely oblivious to my withdrawals. They never even checked it.

That summer, although my friends and I still went out

working during the school holidays, whether it was berry-picking or taking on roofing jobs on local houses, gambling was my major past-time. Having the Manchester United booty available was a real bonus and once, with £100 in my pocket, I persuaded my very good friend, Jon Law – still as close a pal today as he was then – to bring £100 he had saved because I had a full-proof method of beating the bookies. Or so I thought.

We could, I told him, turn our money into £1000 by following the champion jockey, Lester Piggott, and backing all his mounts at Newmarket one Saturday afternoon. It made sense, I insisted.

Jon had earned his money through hard work: labouring, berry-picking and other menial jobs. With other friends we travelled into Elgin and while they went off to the pub, he and I headed for the bookmakers to make our fortune.

My system was so naive and corny, although I didn't think so at the time. We would place £5 on Piggott in his first race and if he lost we would double up to £10 in the next race. If that failed we would go to £20 and so on. It was easy, of course, to very quickly burn a couple of hundred quid. Of Piggott's six mounts that day, none was first past the post. Jon and I exited that bookmakers £200 lighter.

We met up with our pals who had been persuaded we would return as rich men and that we would party into the night on our winnings. In the end, Jon and I got drunk to drown our sorrows. He learned his lesson and became a moderate gambler. Me? I learned nothing and simply chased it for years to come, hoping and believing I could recoup my losses, all my losses. That was pretty serious stuff for a 16-year-old. By the time I was to leave for Manchester United, the Bisto tin was empty and I was well down the road towards a heavy-duty problem that was to follow me for the next 34 years.

4

From Mosstodloch to Manchester

It was July 1975 and the gleaming Mercedes pulled up outside my home in Mosstodloch. The neighbours' curtains twitched and some of the street's urchins gathered round to catch a glimpse of the luxury car, the like of which had never before been seen in the village.

Norman Scholes, Manchester United's chief scout, and Gordon Clayton, his assistant, invited me to place my suitcase in the boot of the vehicle and signalled for me to sit in the back. There were no hugs, no kisses from my parents, just a simple wave and a cheerio and I was on my way to the north-west of England and my club accommodation in the Fallowfield district of Manchester.

I was entering the big world on my own, a world so different from the one I knew and loved, and I was nervous about the challenge ahead. Maybe the club scouts who were so keen to bag my signature sensed that removing me from the idyll of the Highlands would be too big a step. So they put a clause in my contract that, for the first year, they would fly me home once a month after a game on a Saturday and I would return to Manchester on the Tuesday.

It may have prevented me from becoming homesick but I never ever lost my love for my home and the area.

My digs were comfortable. The place was run by a Mr and Mrs Bumby, perfectly nice people who looked after me and the other young professionals they housed.

It was there, a year later, that I was to meet Oshor Williams a talented right winger who was to become a rock for me and a friend to whom I owe so much.

Oshor, from Stockton-on-Tees, is the child of a father from Sierra Leone and an English mother. We would take two buses each morning to the famous Cliff training ground from which Manchester United moved in 2000. As promised, I joined the club as a professional and not as an apprentice and I was paid a weekly wage of £80, around £850 in today's money. I never realised how lucky I was at a time in Britain when, earlier that year, the country's coal miners successfully negotiated a 35 per cent pay rise to take them from £45 to £61 a week. Margaret Thatcher, then plotting to become leader of the Conservative Party, was to punish them when she came to power for what she saw as their greed.

Yet here was I, 17 years old and being handed considerably more than a miner would earn. And there was no polishing the football boots of senior players nor washing the shower-room floors nor sweeping out the dressing rooms.

It was a period of high inflation – 22 per cent – of Evel Kneivel, IRA bombings and the disappearance of Lord Lucan, named by a Coroner's Court as the murderer of his children's nanny, Sandra Rivett.

I was with the Bumbys for about three years before moving to other lodgings, closer to the Cliff, in Salford. They were run by Tom and Annie Kay, who were later to look after some other youngsters who went on to became major stars – David Beckham and Mark Hughes among them.

Tommy Docherty liked attacking formations, and in the first-team squad there were a lot of exciting players to be around. Steve Coppell was on the right and Gordon Hill on the left, both flying wingers; Lou Macari and Sammy McIlroy buzzed around the midfield; Martin Buchan, from Aberdeen, was a star defender; and within two or three years of my joining, Joe Jordan, Ray Wilkins and Gordon McQueen arrived at the club. It was such an exhilarating place, boasting a real mixture of Scots, English and Irish players.

The Doc used to joke that he always promised the chairman of whatever club he managed that he would take the team into another division. He had done that in1974 when he led United from the First to the Second Division, although they bounced back quickly and won promotion to the top league the following season, just in time for me joining.

Stuart Pearson, a burly centre forward, scored 17 league goals that year and Macari, an irascible Scot, scored the goal that clinched promotion at Southampton on 5 April, 1975.

It would not be unfair to state that, in terms of youth development, there wasn't much to brag about in those days at Old Trafford. There was a first-team squad of 18–20 players and a similar sized reserve squad in which I had figured rather quickly after participating with the youth side.

In season 1976–77 I was promoted to the first-team squad and made my debut in October 1976 against Sunderland in a midweek game on a foggy, dreary, drizzly Manchester night. We drew 3–3 and I remember creating one of our goals with a long, diagonal pass. The following Saturday I played against Leicester City away from home and again we drew, this time 1–1. I had another solid game and was in the side the following Wednesday for a League cup-tie against Everton.

It was then that I became acquainted with Bob Latchford, a powerful, physical striker for the Goodison Park club who was my direct opponent. He had joined Everton from Birmingham City in 1974 and the £350,000 transfer fee had made him Britain's most expensive footballer. He was later to win 12 England caps and was excellent in the air and had the ability to score goals from anywhere. To say that he ripped me to shreds that night would be a massive understatement as he scored a hat-trick and we were beaten 4–1.

The Old Trafford crowd must have recognised the Latchford–

Paterson contest for what it was, a man against a boy. I could not match his strength or compete with his power and throughout the drubbing, I kept reminding myself why I much preferred playing up front to being a centre half.

My confidence was shattered. I was a tall lad but couldn't handle Latchford's greater physique and while Martin Buchan, an old-fashioned sweeper, did his best to help and support me, as he did in other games, I simply couldn't handle the beast in the blue jersey. At the time the stadium capacity was over 50,000 and it was a giant leap for me, considering just a couple of seasons earlier I was playing for Jimmy Shanks's team on a Sunday afternoon and in the Highland League on Saturdays.

The Manchester United training was not as sophisticated as it is today. I had been a big, skinny lad and I would have needed a great deal of development work on my upper body if I were to make the grade as a centre half. But there was none of the kind of exercise and gymnasium equipment that is readily available today.

I fell back after the Everton match and didn't figure in the first team until the following season, this time in my preferred role up front. I had developed my own skill from the parks of Moray and I was very much capable of operating in various positions within a team.

Indeed, when I joined Sheffield United in 1980, I was signed as a central midfield player. So, my versatility and usefulness followed me around. I had quick feet, good vision and excellent passing skills, though I admit to having been pretty useless in the air and too one-paced.

There was a culture surrounding football in those days that, because you trained from 10.30 a.m. only for a couple of hours, the rest of the day was your own. You could choose to fill in your time at home or play golf or snooker with some of the lads from the football club.

There was also another option – the bookies – to which I found myself drawn, convinced I would have a winner or two every time I stepped inside. And, as it was not uncommon to have a Wednesday off, you were free from lunchtime on a Tuesday until 10.30 a.m. on the Thursday. That resulted in Tuesday night drinking sessions for many of the playing staff, although I restricted myself to post-match boozing on a Saturday. The midweek knees-up never really appealed to me. The gambling, on the other hand, was a different matter.

Looking back on those days, it was clear that the amount of free time available was not good for young players who should have been encouraged back to the training ground to hone and improve their skills and build their bodies. That was never on offer. I fell into the local gambling culture and I spent most afternoons in the betting shop, along with a few other boys from the reserve squad.

In my second season, my wages rose to £100 a week but with the increase came no guidance or advice on how to save your money or how to manage it. I think a lot of players in those days who finished their careers in their early to mid 30s struggled with life after football because they had no idea how to handle their money. Neither had they many social skills or a trade or profession on which they could fall back. Everything had been done for them by the football club and so they had difficulty organising their own lives. At the end of their careers they were ill-equipped for the real world. I knew a few who were lost and who hit hard times and I felt for them.

My obsession with gambling was as unhealthy as it was uncontrollable. We were paid weekly on a Friday and after paying for my lodgings – around £15 – I had only food and transport costs to deal with. That left me with plenty of spare cash for betting and, without fail, I would lose it all early on in the week. Every week.

I also had a love affair with cards, an accepted part of the football world as we travelled to away games. Today, footballers on the team bus might be engrossed in listening to their iPods, trawling the internet on their laptops, chatting on their mobile phones or even reading books and magazines. In our time it was quite straightforward; you might like to read a book, like Martin Buchan would, but it was more than likely you would be part of a group of players engaged in a card school at the back of the bus for fairly serious money.

There were also the Monday evening poker games attended by some of the more serious card sharps when big money often changed hands and tension would sometimes hang heavy in the air. It was through those occasions that I forged a good friendship with Kevin Moran, a top player in his day, who liked nothing better than a game of poker. Generally speaking the stakes weren't too high. It was more of a recreational evening. At least, that's how some of us chose to label it.

Kevin, a tough, uncompromising centre-half, yet only 5ft 10in tall, had the heart of a lion and was to become a cult hero at Manchester United. He had joined the club at the relatively late age of 21 from league football in the Republic of Ireland, where he was already a big hero, having won All-Ireland Gaelic football championships.

He and I became good friends in his early years when he was finding his feet in the reserve team and, being Irish, he liked a pint of Guinness: a man after my own heart. I used to look forward to him going home on occasional breaks as he always returned with bottles of Poteen, the illicit moonshine made from potatoes that was an incredibly powerful brew.

Mind you, he didn't just drink the stuff. He would also rub it on his legs as a healer of injuries. Remarkably, it worked.

The most common of his injuries, however, were cuts to his head, all down to his fearlessness and his willingness to put that part of his body in where it hurt. He must have chalked-up hundreds of stitches to head wounds and invariably found himself a principal member of the walking wounded around Old Trafford.

Kevin was one of football's great pranksters and when he first arrived from Ireland his lodgings were in the Chorlton area, where the family had theatrical links. It was there that he came across a couple of police uniforms and he and another young player from Ireland would dress up and, with torch lights, would beckon passing motorists to the side of the road and question them on whether they had been drinking. Recognising their fear and nervousness, he would, in his strong Irish brogue, warn them to be extra careful and watch them squirm and sweat and swear blind they hadn't been drinking as they thought they were about to be breathalysed and charged.

One day, Kevin and I 'stole' Gary Bailey's car from the Cliff training ground. We acquired his car keys after training and started up the vehicle before the big South African arrived on the scene.

He wasn't pleased and we goaded him by opening the passenger door then driving off just as he attempted to get in. He followed us down Broughton Road but after several repeats of moving away as he tried to board, his patience snapped and he marched off back to the training ground.

Kevin and I chuckled at our schoolboy prank and drove Gary's car over to Old Trafford. Its owner, however, was to have the last laugh by reporting to the police that his car had been stolen. Next day, we were summoned to the office of Dave Sexton, our new boss after Tommy Docherty had been sacked, and given a severe dressing down and fined for our trouble.

If my gambling was becoming problematic – and it clearly was – I failed to recognise it. I enjoyed the buzz of the bookmaker's and the cut and thrust of the card schools, so why wouldn't I thrill at the prospect of attending the greyhound racing at Bell Vue?

And there was also White City, another great venue for Manchester's dog-racing fraternity. Those places were a magnet for me and I was punting on the dogs up to three nights a week.

I read a funny tale in the autobiography of Niall Quinn, a star centre-forward at Arsenal and Manchester City and a great hero at Sunderland, where he later became chairman. He was a 'mug punter' who would go to the dog tracks and hide his bus fare behind a lamppost outside to ensure he had money to get his way home if, as usually happened, he lost everything.

I never had the foresight to stick this 'insurance' aside and can recall several occasions when I trudged home penniless from Bell Vue.

5

Going to the dogs, and Salad days

My old friend Jon Law, who had moved to Manchester a year after I did, and another pal, Steve Kelly, were studying to be teachers at the De La Salle College of Education in Manchester. Steve was president of the students' union, and his Irish father Joe was a well-known greyhound trainer in Leeds. As a means of supplementing their meagre education grants, they would 'borrow' one of Steve's dad's top dogs and enter it in open races throughout the country. I was so taken with dog racing that I was determined to get in on the action, even though many of our 'raids' would end in disaster when what we thought was a safe bet would choose to have an off-night or simply be beaten by faster dogs.

There was one adventure, however, that proved successful. Steve produced a winner he had been preparing for months for a major open race at Wimbledon. His father was sweet on its chances because it had been winning local races in Leeds. The Wimbledon meeting was on a Thursday night in November and because the Manchester United squad always had an easy training session over at Old Trafford on a Friday morning, and I didn't want to miss out on the dog-racing action, I decided to travel south with Jon and Steve.

Steve saw it as part of his role as the students' president to advise his colleagues when a 'sure thing' was running to allow them to make an investment of their savings or grants. His 'sure thing' on this occasion was a dog called Prince Hill. In the build-up to the trip, Steve collected the dog from Leeds and took it back to his flat in Swinton so that it could relax for a couple of days. Prince Hill was treated like canine royalty, with its own bedroom and the best steaks money could buy.

On the day of the race, Steve picked me up from training in his battered old blue Avenger car and as he drove and Jon occupied the front passenger seat, Prince and I spread ourselves as best we could along the back seat. We had a barrow-load of money to place – stakes of £5, £10 and £20 on behalf of students and lecturers at De La Salle, all their names written alongside their individual bets. I had managed to gather £200 – a couple of week's wages – and, as usual, I was as excited as could be at the prospect of a massive win.

Once at the track, Steve's job was to get Prince Hill organised for his big moment, while Jon and I split up, and from opposite ends of the long row of bookmakers we punted the money in small amounts so as not to arouse suspicion that we had a winner. After all, that would only alert other punters, which would bring down the dog's odds.

Unlike us, the bookies were no mugs and were used to visitors from the north trying to fleece them in such a manner. They would also have a network of spies around the country to advise them of the potential of visiting dogs. Soon, the price available of 6/1 when we began working our way from bookie to bookie was chopped to to 3/1 before we had even finished placing our bets. Still, even at those tighter odds, if Prince could fulfil our hopes, we would do well.

As the traps opened, our greyhound, wearing the stripes of No. 6, came out like a bolt of lightning and led all the way round the two circuits of the race. He won by a healthy four lengths.

An ecstatic Jon and I could see Steve jumping with joy at the finishing line. What a sting. What a feeling; a mixture of scoring a winning goal and having passionate sex. Such emotions were cementing my lifetime addiction.

We collected our winnings from a line of bookmakers who

were, to put it mildly, pissed off, and we departed Wimbledon on cloud nine. We needed a beer to celebrate and time to count the cash and, by pure coincidence, we stopped at a pub in Twickenham, ironically called The Greyhound.

For once, I was sensible and settled for a couple of pints of Guinness and volunteered to drive back to Manchester. En route, we visited a Chinese restaurant, ordering Oriental dishes for us, and double steak and chips for Prince Hill. When we had enjoyed a good feed we headed home a very happy trio of punters. Steve had our prize asset across his lap in the back seat of the Avenger, and sang lullabies to the Prince all the way home.

In the front, beside Jon, was a holdall packed with banknotes – £5000 worth of them – and considering it was £1000 more than an annual salary for a schoolteacher and the equivalent of around £25,000 in today's money, it was a not inconsiderable haul.

I slipped into Annie and Tom's at 5 a.m. and grabbed a couple of hours' sleep before Old Trafford training that morning and felt rather pleased with myself with more than £1000 of winnings in my pocket.

Occasions like those were, of course, rare. My experiences of so-called 'good things' or tips have been generally bad. Being 'in the know' has only rarely worked for me. I was once involved in a racehorse a group of Manchester United players had purchased as a syndicate. It was trained by David 'The Duke' Nicholson, one of the great jump trainers of modern times.

Lou Macari, never averse to seeking the main chance in the betting stakes, had many friends in the racing business and he, too, was part of the syndicate which bought the horse, named Salad. It was a topic of conversation at training when it was scheduled to run and Lou would give us updates on its chances. The plan was to map it out for a race at Haydock and give the bookies a caning.

It ran a few races at places like Uttoxeter and Huntingdon

where it was gently schooled and never put out to win, usually ending up well down the field. This meant that with no form to its name, its odds would lengthen with each outing.

One day, we received the word that it was ready to win at Uttoxeter, where it was entered in a poor race. Along with a few players from the reserves, I drove across to the racetrack itching to be in on the sting.

Unfortunately, being a mug punter without a modicum of self-discipline, I could not wait for Salad's race at 4 p.m. I was experiencing a bad day, not just with bets at Uttoxeter, but with those on horses at other courses throughout the land. By 4 p.m. I was broke, even though I had already borrowed money from some of the other lads. The stake money I had set out for Salad was gone and, surprise, surprise, our horse raced home as a 12/1 winner. I was furious with myself that I had been so reckless before the race even started.

The scenario was exacerbated a few days later when we were travelling to Marbella for a golfing break. I had hardly two ha'pennies to rub together while Lou carried a bag which, I was told, had the £10,000 winnings, courtesy of Salad, ready to be distributed to the lucky punters in the squad.

Despite that, I enjoyed Marbella and perked up when Gordon McQueen gifted me a set of golf clubs after taking pity on me when he discovered my disaster with Salad.

The next opportunity to make money from the horse's efforts proved even more catastrophic. It was at Haydock and we were told it was a certainty to win. I had no money and so I made an appointment with my bank manager, himself a punter and one with whom I shared tips. I shared with him my secret about Salad and he allowed me to borrow £5000 – put through as a two-year loan for a car – and I was happy that I had a sufficient sum to make my fortune and see me repay the loan the day after the race.

This time, though, I chose not to attend the race as I didn't want to be tempted by the on-course bookies to part with money before the main event. Instead, feeling like Mr 'Big-Time', I went into Manchester city centre with the £5000 in my training bag and spread my bets around various bookies as vast sums would not have been accepted at one place.

This was to be a magic moment for me – my biggest-ever stake.

My heart was pumping harder and faster than ever and my hands were sweating at the prospect of gathering up my fortune at the end of the race. The thought of losing never even entered my head.

My fate was sealed early on in the race, however, as Salad fell at the third fence. My £5000 was down the river in under a minute and I would be paying for it for two years. Non-gamblers may not be able to comprehend such stupidity. Nor would they be able to come to terms with the fact that a chronic gambler cannot accept such drastic losses as a warning never to place another bet.

Despite what punters may say, there is no such thing as a 'cert'. The father-in-law of Barry Wilson, who played for me when I was manager at Inverness Caledonian Thistle, owned a horse called Kyle of Lochalsh which, despite Barry's tips, I always resisted backing. Often, when it was backed into short odds and favouritism, I would recall Barry's description of it as 'running as if pulling a caravan'. Barry, himself a flyer, would have outpaced Kyle of Lochalsh. Come to think of it, his father-in-law would probably have given it a good run for its money as well.

6

Annie, Tom and lazy Sundays

In Manchester, I didn't want to admit to myself that my habit was taking a real hold. It was 1977, I was still not 19 years old and I was losing heavily and drifting deeper into debt. On top of that, the losses and debts were preying so heavily on my mind that my football started to suffer and pretty soon I was turning up for a game on a Saturday having lost my week's wages less than 24 hours earlier. I shudder to think how I would have coped mentally had I been married and had greater responsibilities.

I did, though, have a girlfriend, called Karen Anderson. We had been childhood sweethearts at Milne's High School and she had moved to Manchester to train as a nurse. Karen had picked up quite early on that my gambling was out of control because of the number of times I had borrowed money from her – money which I regularly lost at the casino just down the road from my lodgings with Tom and Annie Kay in Lower Broughton Road.

The close proximity of the casino – just 10 minutes' walk away – meant that I was soon in the grip of what was, for me, a new form of gambling. Like all forms of betting, there are good days and bad. Ultimately, of course, it will all lead to debt and despair. I now had a three-pronged addiction to contend with; after training I would head to the betting shops or one of the many racetracks around Manchester; evenings might be spent at Bell Vue greyhounds or local 'flapping' tracks; and for my dessert course it would be the Salford casino until 4 a.m. Little wonder I never reached my full potential. My relationship with Karen was also suffering.

Oshor Williams, returning to the area with Stockport County after a couple of seasons at Southampton following his release from United, also moved in to Annie and Tom's place. Actually, we played against each other at the Dell, Southampton's previous home – they are at St Mary's now – and drew 1–1.

Oshor and I shared a room at the digs and forged a great friendship which lasts to this day. But how he put up with me says a great deal about his tolerance and loyalty, especially as deceit was now playing a bigger role in my character as my gambling became more firmly entrenched and I was even stealing to satisfy my habit. Osh could always read me like a book and would constantly pick over my bogus stories of where I had been and what I had done with my money.

Sometimes, when I was late back for dinner, Oshor, Annie and Tom and their children, Dave and Gill, would sit in the living room and watch me trudge up Lower Broughton Road towards the house. They never failed to detect by the way I walked that it had been a day of losses for me. My head would be bowed and my pace would be slow and funereal.

Often, when I was desperate and on a losing streak, I would return from the casino in the middle of the night, tiptoe into our bedroom and rummage through Oshor's belongings in his bedside drawer for the cash I knew he kept in a box. Then I would return to the casino for further punishment until closing time at 4 a.m. having lost my best friend's hard-earned wages.

'For fuck's sake Steve,' he would bawl at me the following day when he heard my confession, 'when are you going to learn that you can't win? You need help.'

I would agree and make the usual pledges and promises. In truth, the cycle of behaviour continued and it was more than 30 years before I did seek help.

Such tales may paint a picture of abject misery, but my time with Annie and Tom was far from unhappy. We were treated as members of the family and Annie was regarded as the queen of landladies, with Sundays in particular being supremely special days. It was then that Oshor, Tom, Dave and I would be in the local pub by midday to enjoy a pint of marvellous Boddington's beer and a game of cribbage – for money, of course.

At three o'clock we would return to the house, where Annie and Gill would have prepared the most wonderful Sunday roast. An hour later it was siesta time, and we would sleep until around 7 p.m. when we would be wakened for tea and sandwiches. When we finished, we headed for a second round of cribbage down the pub an hour later. This was a ritual followed by all the Salford lads who drank there, all Manchester United fans and working-class folk, just like me. I doubt if 'Becks' and 'Sparky' Hughes would have kept this tradition going when their time came to move in with Annie and Tom. By the time those stars of the future arrived at Old Trafford, the diet of a footballer had improved dramatically and no way would they have been down at the local bar drinking with the punters.

During my time, on the other hand, the Sunday session was almost compulsory for most players and a dozen pints of 'Boddy's' was pretty much the norm. Come to think of it, all the bad habits I adopted at Manchester United remained with me, especially a good Sunday drink which I enjoyed in later years at the Garmouth Hotel.

I was pleased to see Annie and the late Tom honoured by Sir Alex Ferguson, the United manager, in 2007 when she retired as 'mum' to all the many players who lodged with her over a period of more than 30 years. The family still maintains friendships with lots of the lads and travelled with Beckham to Madrid and Milan as well as having attended countless weddings of their 'boys'.

Annie and Tom were a largely unheralded component of the United machine and a big part of the United family. I think I probably still owe Anne digs money.

7

Unusual company en route to Wembley

Like most of the other young lads arriving at the Cliff each morning, I was in awe of Tommy Docherty, a charismatic character whose gruff Scottish accent and abrasive nature could rub people up the wrong way. He was always full of life and frequently humorous but the players had a fear of him and knew they could not get too close to the boss. If you were in with him you were OK. If you crossed him, pity help you. He could be ruthless and sharp-tongued but he was the one who had signed me and saw me as a young prospect with an ability to do well for him.

I was in his FA Cup final squad against Southampton in 1976 but didn't make it into the 14 players – 11 plus 3 substitutes in those days – who were on duty that day at Wembley. We lost 1–0 to a Bobby Stokes goal seven minutes from the end.

I was in two more cup final squads but was never one of the 14 stripped for action. Still, the experience was tremendous, especially when we won the FA Cup by beating Liverpool 2–1 the following year, destroying the Merseyside team's aspiration of winning the treble. They won the League Championship and the European Cup on either side of our victory at Wembley, a memorable occasion known as the five-minute final because all three goals came in a period of five spectacular and dramatic minutes. For a young and aspiring professional footballer like me, however, the journey to Manchester en route for Wembley was rather unorthodox.

As it was the end of the season, I had been given permission to return home to Scotland but was under strict instructions to report to Old Trafford at 4 p.m. on the eve of the game, when a large party of players, club staff, their families and friends would gather and then be taken to London on a specially-chartered train.

I could bring a guest, I was told, and offered Donald Macaulay, the husband of my sister Morag and a very good friend as well as a Liverpool fan, the opportunity to rub shoulders with some of British football's greatest players of the time and to sit with me in the VIP section at Wembley stadium.

In the heady and luxurious atmosphere of being a member of the first team squad of a major world football club, travel arrangements, even for those not included in the playing squad, would be first class. Had I been in that position today and been earning mega money, say £30,000-a-week – not uncommon for fringe players in the modern game – I could have hired a private jet to ferry Donald and me south. In the 1970s, though, despite coining it, I was always broke and my brother-in-law, then head of physical education at a private school, was saving hard to buy a home for the first time for him and Morag. In other words, we couldn't afford the fare from Mosstodloch to London. So, we turned to the only option available . . . we hitch-hiked to the FA Cup final of 1977.

Dressed in my striped cup final suit, with its club crest on the breast pocket and flared trousers, I set off with Donald shortly after midnight on Thursday, giving us sufficient time to reach Manchester by the appointed hour. We knew in our hearts that it would not all be plain sailing and that we would have to walk for spells.

Still, our sojourn started well. We hadn't even crossed the boundary of Fochabers when, in the main street, we flagged down a large lorry belonging to the Baxters food company.

'Any chance of a lift, mate?' In for a penny, in for a pound, I thought.

'Sorry pal,' answered the driver. 'We're not allowed. Insurance and all that.'

'Come on. We're heading for the English cup final. Look,' I took the breast of my jacket in between a finger and thumb to show him my badge. 'I play for Manchester United.'

'Aye, sure . . . and you're hitch-hiking?'

'Skint.'

The friendly driver shook his head and thought for a moment. 'I'm only going as far as Glasgow. Jump in.'

We were on our way, crushed into the cab of the big truck, but with a hospitable driver who was good company all the way and ready to allow us to share his flask of tea. Reaching the outskirts of Glasgow was a relief, and Donald and I parted from the huge lorry with sore backs and thoughts of where and when we would find our next lift. We set off on foot and silently prayed for a Good Samaritan in a spacious and comfortable up-market car who would whisk us straight to our destination.

We walked for what seemed like an eternity, hugging the hard shoulder of the motorway and trying to be seen in the dark. I held out my holdall with its luminous stripes, hoping a friendly motorist would take pity on us. In time we came across an all-night service station where we could assess our progress and address important matters, like finding something to eat and cadging a lift from a sympathetic trucker. Inside, we comforted ourselves with hot tea and Scotch pies and sat next to a burly, ruddy-complexioned man wearing a grubby, checked cap.

'Aye, aye,' he said. 'Fit like?'

A friendly voice from the depths of Aberdeenshire, spluttered out his greeting. We might just have struck gold, I thought. Our conversation included the usual questions. Where are you from? Where are you going? He knew nothing about nor had an interest in football, but when we mentioned our predicament he gave us the response we wanted to hear.

'You're welcome to a lift in my lorry. It's a wee bit rough and ready, like, but I'm sure you'll nae be bithered aboot 'at.'

Indeed not. After fifteen minutes of chewing the fat, making more small talk, and endeavouring to ignore his overwhelming body odour, this man with callus-covered hands the size of shovels told us he was going as far as Kendal, in the Lake District, and, as we walked out into the car park, he pointed to his vehicle and signalled that we should hoist ourselves into the cabin.

Donald and I looked at each other. Had beggars been choosers we might just have thanked this loon for the offer and returned to the canteen for a second mug of tea and waited for another opportunity. We could not afford to be so blasé, however, and so we joined our driver and God knows how many mooing, farting, smelly cows in the back of a cattle truck headed for a livestock market.

The lorry must have been ten years old as it clattered its way towards the border. The ventilation was nonexistent and our farmhand friend's pong worsened with each passing hour as the atmosphere inside grew stickier because of the heat from the engine. His personal smell almost, but not quite, overpowered the stench of his cargo and the rattling of the ancient truck and the constant groans from behind us, did not make for a pleasant or comfortable trip.

There were long silences during which Donald and I, as we discovered later when he compared notes, thought along the same lines – when the fuck are we going to reach Kendal?

Aberdeenshire Alex – his name was Sandy – had clearly not been acquainted with soap or water for some considerable time, but he was cheery and unworldly and strangely likeable. More importantly, he played his part in helping us reach our destination and in the end I felt bad that we couldn't even afford to give him a bung for his trouble. Every penny we had, and there weren't many, would be needed for our Wembley weekend.

Whether it was the smell of Sandy or his travelling companions, a foul stench seemed to stay in my nostrils throughout the following stage of our journey and must have surprised our next chauffeur, a self-employed joiner going straight to Manchester.

Like a boxer who pulls back when he has just had smelling salts placed under his nose, our new driver, Tommo, blanched when we joined him in the front seat of his Transit van.

'Fook's sake,' he growled in his northern accent, 'can't say ah think mooch o' yer after-shave.'

Tommo laughed uproariously when we told him we'd just shared several hours with a herd of cows and a driver who'd never in his life been near a bottle of eau de toilette. His van was sheer luxury compared to our previous mode of transport and he was good enough to drop us within a few miles of Old Trafford, where Donald and I were able to shower, freshen up and take a damp cloth to some of the stains we'd picked up on our clothes during our adventure.

Soon, we were on our way as part of a large Manchester United party ready to support the Reds on this gala occasion, the FA Cup final, always a carnival day in the calendar of any football club.

Once we arrived in London it was five-star facilities all the way and, while I had made Donald promise not to react if Liverpool scored, I practically had to sit on him to curb his enthusiasm when Jimmy Case equalised after Stuart Pearson had opened the scoring for United. Then Lou Macari's strike was deflected off the chest of team-mate Jimmy Greenhoff and into Ray Clemence's net to give us the FA Cup. What a day and what a night.

We missed the post-match banquet but joined in the celebrations and even spent time 'interviewing' TV football pundit Jimmy Hill about BBC's coverage of Scottish football. Then, it was off on a coach with all the Old Trafford players, now with the pressure valve having been opened, singing their heads off as they enjoyed the fruits of their labour.

Just forty-four days after that cup triumph, however, the Doc's four-and-a-half-year stay at Manchester United ended. He was sacked when it emerged that he was having an affair with Mary, the wife of the club physiotherapist, Laurie Brown. Tommy and Mary were later to marry and, in true Docherty style, they faced the world with pride and defiance. On being told by the United board that his £20,000 a year contract, which still had 10 months to run, was being terminated, the Doc had this to say: 'I'm a bit shattered. I certainly didn't expect this. It was a bombshell. I thought I would have been judged on my playing record, like Wembley in two successive years.'

He was soon back in work, with Derby County, where his tenure lasted a couple of years before he headed for Queen's Park Rangers but, when he failed to win them promotion to the First Division, he was shown the door. Ironically, our paths were to cross once more several years later when I baby-sat Tommy and Mary's children on the other side of the world.

Credit cards were not on the financial scene in the 1970s. If you needed extra money you went, cap in hand, to your bank manager and dreamt up a reason for requiring a loan. I was forced to see my bank manager quite often for one so young, as I had discovered that the private bookies – those faceless men on the end of a telephone who would take your big-money bets – didn't like to wait too long for their cash.

Sure, there was the euphoria of a massive win, perhaps a five-figure sum, but it was always followed by a loss, no matter what. It was like a kind of madness. There was never going to be a meaningful ending. I was simply funding my addiction. Did I recognise that at the time? No. I was constantly skint. A betting shop to me was like a toy shop to a child.

My versatility as a player paid off at Old Trafford because I was useful to have in the squad. I had been offered a new deal on the basis that a player like me, a squad player, was good to have around.

I was seen as a guy who would go places, a first-team regular and maybe even an international player of the future. This potential was underlined when I was named in Andy Rox-burgh's Scotland under-21 squad for a European Championship match in Czechoslovakia in 1976.

I was proud to have been called up by my country, especially for the first under-21 match Scotland had played. Prior to 1976, the age group was under-23. But I did feel sometimes as if I didn't belong where I was. I thought: I'm a boy from a wee village in the north of Scotland. What the hell am I doing at Manchester United and being pressed into international duty?

My problem, if indeed it was that, was that I was never ambitious. Things just happened to me. For all that, I thoroughly enjoyed training and the camaraderie that accompanied it.

Under Docherty, sessions were hard but often packed with fun. His assistant, Tommy Cavanagh, on the other hand, could be a nightmare to work with and when the bush telegraph informed us that some of the first-team squad were injured and unable to train, we would lock ourselves in the toilets of the reserve team dressing room – sometimes five to a cubicle – to escape being dragooned to make up the numbers and participate in the top team's sessions. If you weren't quick you were left to the mercy of Cav.

It wasn't that we didn't want to be with stars like Alex Stepney, Ray Wilkins, Joe Jordan and the others. It was because Cavanagh, a straight-talking Scouser, would take no prisoners in his criticism, usually delivered at the top of his voice for all to hear. Such behaviour was too much to bear from a man with a fearsome tongue and the toughest of natures. Apart from any-thing else, his aggressive style was counter-productive and scared the living daylights out of young players who were apprehensive about getting on the ball in case they made a mistake and were on the receiving end of a Cavanagh bollicking.

Give us the more acceptable sessions run by Frank Blunstone, Jack Crompton, Jimmy Curran and the great Harry Gregg, the goalkeeper who was one of the survivors of the Manchester United European Cup side involved in the Munich air disaster in 1958. Frank, Jack, Jimmy and Harry were all coaches with whom we enjoyed working.

Some of the United heroes in the top team would frequently see the youngsters as fodder for their humour and pranks. Lou Macari dubbed me Big Bird because of my full head of curly black hair, which he thought resembled a bird's nest. The nickname ended up as Big Bud and it stuck. I certainly wasn't Pele at Old Trafford – though I was still Pele back home.

The jokes and jibes at my expense were all good fun and no offence was taken. All I could think was that I was the luckiest lad in the world, coming from a little Scots village, a dot on the map, and now part of one of the biggest football clubs on the planet.

As time wore on, however, I came to accept that I wasn't quite good enough for that level. I didn't have the required pace and while I had a good football brain and talent, I knew that I would be better suited to football one level below, in Division Two.

When Docherty left and was replaced by Dave Sexton, an extremely pleasant man with impeccable manners, I was still a member of the first team squad and by then on £200 a week. To put my riches into context, the average weekly wage for a man was less than £50 while for women it was £27.

Sexton, who had previously been in charge at QPR, was a different type of manager and was seen as a modern coach with fresh, innovative training methods. He was quiet, unassuming and extremely likeable. In his first two seasons the club finished no better than tenth in the league campaign, and I turned out for the first team a few times, at Tottenham and at Arsenal and other grounds as well as at Old Trafford. Sexton also led us to another FA Cup final. Once more I was part of the travelling party, and once more I was to face disappointment by being excluded from those who walked out on to the manicured Wembley turf.

I was beginning to think that I no longer wished to continue as a bit-part player with the Reds and that I wanted to perform every week. By then, I was part of a group of international players from the Home Nations, like Gordon McQueen, Steve Coppell, Mickey Thomas and Jimmy Nicholl. Yet, I could not envisage becoming a first-team regular, although for a manager I was the ideal squad player because of my versatility. I decided, after five seasons to move on.

Sexton's offer of a further three-year contract fell on deaf ears and when news leaked that I might be available for transfer, other clubs started to sniff around a player who was attractive to them because he had sampled first team action in the First Division with one of its best sides and who had experienced European football – albeit as a substitute – against high calibre outfits like Ajax and Juventus.

When Sheffield United offered £80,000 for my transfer – that would make me a £700,000 player today – the deal was done. As part of it I was to be given a house, rent-free, a car and, more importantly, a sizeable signing-on fee. That was crucial because by then I was in hock to the bookies to the tune of about £5000. In short, I needed that move to Bramall Lane, the home of Sheffield United, where, under manager Harry Haslam, I could establish myself as a first team player. Unfortunately, that was never going to be the case. My dream move turned into a nightmare and I was dubbed 'the ghost of Bramall Lane' by the Blades fans. They were never to witness their new star signing from the mighty Manchester United.

8

The ghost of Bramall Lane

It was the summer of 1980 and I was excited about the future. But there was a snag.

Towards the end of the previous season I had picked up an ankle injury which didn't trouble me too much. Only a week or two into my pre-season training with the Blades, however, and I broke down. The alarm bells started ringing with Haslam and his coaching staff. The injury failed to respond to treatment and questions were now being asked. Had they bought damaged goods? Had they bought a dud?

Sheffield United had paid a £20,000 deposit on my transfer fee but, concerned that they now had a player who wasn't going to be able to play, they started immediate negotiations with Manchester United to cancel the deal.

I was moved out of the flat they had provided me with while talks took place and the signing-on fee was put on hold. This was bad news and it took around six months for an agreement to be reached between the clubs that one United would return the £20,000 to the other. Meanwhile, I sat on the sidelines and, without a roof of my own over my head, I slept on Steve Kelly's couch back in Manchester.

By this time Steve had moved a couple of top greyhounds into his house as permanent residents and, as they had priority, Jon and I, both sharing the accommodation, were not afforded a bed. In essence we were second-class citizens compared to the dogs who always ate the best steaks while we settled for chips and gravy.

Jon and I used to receive a benefits Giro through the post on a Friday morning and have it gambled away by lunchtime. Times were hard. We would sell off personal belongings to a local pawn shop and even removed some of Steve's items of furniture when we became really desperate for cash.

In time, the wrangling between Manchester United and Sheffield United was over and I was encouraged to retire from football, at least in the UK, in order for the insurance company to pay out the required compensation of £80,000. The transfer had now collapsed.

I was deeply disappointed. A period of rest and treatment, I felt, would have fixed the problem. I had a much bigger concern, though; I needed a hefty sum of money to get those private bookies off my back and without the lump sum I was to receive from the deal, I was in trouble.

Eventually, I agreed to walk away and officially accept that my injury would not permit me ever again to participate in league football anywhere in the UK. I would be rewarded with a five-figure sum which allowed me to settle my debts and, of course, build new ones.

Looking back, Manchester might be described as a negative part of my life as it firmly established my gambling habit. Had I been in a normal nine-to-five job it might have been different. I needed my time to be more structured, although it probably wouldn't have prevented the inevitable. The addictive gene in me would have surfaced, no matter what.

I hadn't realised just how destructive my gambling had become. It definitely ruined my career at that level as I accepted premature retirement in order to pay off my debtors. I should have enjoyed a lengthy career in English league football.

But I feel fortunate and privileged that I had a five-year period with one of the world's biggest football brands. I may have started only a half dozen games and come on as a substitute for a similar number of others, but I had some fabulous experiences, in particular a three-week pre-season tour of Canada and the United States. Martin Buchan and I shared a room and he took me under his wing. He was a steadying influence – or at least he tried to be. The game was attempting to get off the ground on the other side of the Atlantic and we were there to try to help its progress.

We started off against Vancouver Whitecaps, then Chicago Bears and the Dallas Cowboys. After it all we had a week in Bermuda to rest.

Then there were the memorable European ties and an involvement with a group of hugely-talented footballers. What a life: playing football for a good living and, in my free time, indulging in my favourite pastime of gambling. I felt invincible and I had no long-term vision. I lived for the moment and was carefree. I was never serious enough about football and often felt uncomfortable that I was part of something in which I didn't belong.

I could and should have been a great deal more dedicated, but gambling was more important than football. Gambling was what influenced my mood and attitude, while football was there simply to fund it. Gambling took me over from an early age.

As I lodged with Steve, I had been going through a rough patch with my girlfriend Karen. She grew increasingly tired of my financially-debilitating habit. She had taken a job at Edinburgh Royal Infirmary at the conclusion of her nursing course and we both saw that move as a chance for a fresh start for our relationship.

We agreed that I would spend a few days in the Scottish capital and that we should have a holiday in the sun somewhere. She chose the destination – Tenerife – and I saw the vacation as an opportunity to consider my future and to rekindle the love I had felt for her.

The £600 which she had set aside for the break was in her possession for safe-keeping. One morning, as she was leaving the house to start a day shift, she informed me that the holiday cash was on the mantelpiece. Would I go to the travel agent and pay for the holiday she had booked? If ever there was trust and confidence shown in me, this was it. Was she mad?

My immediate thoughts were that I would double the money. I felt excited and the adrenalin pumped through my body as I entered a little betting shop pledging to 'give them a doing' on this bright, sunny Edinburgh day. My early bets were gentle, £20 and £30 stakes. I had arrived well before the first race in order to study form before stepping up to the counter with my initial line. I felt on top of the world having a stash of money in my pocket and could not countenance even the possibility of failure.

Our holiday might be of the package variety but when I was finished with this bookmaker we would be enjoying the extras my winnings would bring – champagne, the best of restaurants, the works.

The first race started at two o'clock. By the time it would take to play a football match – ninety minutes – I was down to £300. I hadn't backed one winner. Never mind, I thought,

I'd been here before and come through. And, anyway, I still had £300 available. There was no way in the world that I wouldn't be successful.

The situation went from bad to worse. I had a bad case of 'seconditis'. Almost every horse I backed came in immediately behind the winner. Pretty soon I was down to the last £100 and I was desperate, sweating and agitated at the thought of losing it all and seeing the holiday, not to say my relationship with Karen, go down the drain. By then, I was even planning my getaway. Like the coward that I was, my thoughts turned to doing a runner to friends in Manchester rather than face Karen with the news that I had blown all the money she had worked so hard for. Whatever she and I had between us, it was now on the line.

Karen had witnessed my gambling addiction at close hand over a period of years in Manchester. She had listened to my countless promises to give it up. I would change my ways, I always assured her. But every time I made those pledges I knew deep down in my heart that I couldn't shake off my terrible habit. My gambling had a firm hold on me and my lying became second nature.

How could Karen believe that I could walk to a travel agent with £600 in my pocket and not divert to the nearest bookie?

The last race, at 5 p.m., was about to start. I was down to the last £100 and I reverted to a ritual I had turned to many times before – I prayed to God for help. I needed £600 to save my neck. So, I looked for a 6/1 shot, any 6/1 bet, caring not about the form of the horse. Any horse would do as long as it carried those odds. Luck smiled on me – though at the time, in my desperate mind, I believed God had dug me out of my hole, providing deliverance to the tune of £600 plus my £100 stake.

Oh happy day. Hallelujah! I was in heaven and euphoric. I tipped the bookie £20, a habit I always followed after a decent win, and I skipped out of that betting shop. I had got out of jail this time. With a feeling of relief washing over me, nothing else mattered at that sweet moment.

I went straight to the travel agent, arriving just before closing time, and with the biggest smile on my face, handed over the money for our holiday. I was buzzing when I met Karen a little later. I felt so in love with her and with life. Isn't it remarkable what a win on the horses does for you?

We went to a pub in the Grassmarket for a celebratory drink and, naturally, I lied about my day. I had paid for the holiday first, I told her, then piddled about town, spending half an hour in the bookies where I got lucky and won £50. I had learned always to 'cut' my winnings by half when relaying news of them to Karen. As usual, deceit was second nature to me.

9

Norway no more . . . Hello Hong Kong

At the age of 22 I was finished with the professional game in this country. Any club signing me would have had to pay back in full the £80,000 insurance money. I had no skills other than football so I kept myself fit and thought that if I was to get a living out of the game, it would have to be abroad.

In the meantime, I contacted Aberdeen over the summer of 1981 to request training facilities and Sir Alex Ferguson, the manager at that time, kindly allowed me to do a great deal of pre-season work as I endeavoured to keep up my fitness levels in the event that a club would come along.

I was then invited for a trial period with Dundee United by their manager, Jim McLean, who was keen to assess me. When I informed him that my insurance pay-off stopped me from participating in league football, however, and that should I sign on at Tannadice they would have to re-pay the £80,000, the interest ended.

My appearance in those days took on a rather bizarre look. I had grown a huge handlebar moustache to complement my big, curly mop of hair and I was driving around in a white vintage Ford Popular, circa 1958. It occurred to me later that Sir Alex and Jim Mclean must have had a collective thought along the lines of: 'What fucking planet does he belong to?'

Who would have thought that a little over 20 years later, both clubs would have been seeking this eccentric-looking Highlander as their manager?

Out of the blue I was offered the opportunity to sign for the

Norwegian club, Bryne FK and I was invited to that town, north of Stavanger, to meet with club officials.

Bryne had reached the top league and Brian Green, an Englishman, was the coach there. He had remembered me from my Old Trafford days.

I was to go over for three weeks on trial and they liked what they saw of me and offered me a deal. It was a part-time club and I was to be given a job as a wireless operator, for some reason. They insisted the job was crucial as it was the only way I could get a work permit.

I was delighted to be back in the game at a reasonably high level and it was agreed that I would return to Britain, collect my belongings and return to Norway at the start of the season for a couple of years.

I flitted aimlessly between Moray and Manchester and before setting off for a new life in Bryne I visited friends in the latter where I borrowed a very smart leather holdall in preparation for my Scandinavian adventure. I could not have foreseen the events which followed.

Karen agreed to join me on the flight to Norway. She wanted to see Bryne and spend a long weekend with me as I settled in. We were excited and happy on our arrival in Stavanger, anticipating a fresh beginning for my football career in a new country. Soon after, our joy was to turn sour.

The borrowed holdall was one with numerous zipped compartments and when I arrived in Norway and went through customs, they found a little piece of silver foil. Inside the foil was a small quantity of cannabis. I may have enjoyed alcohol and gambling but I had never dabbled in drugs. Guinness and red wine were my sources of relaxation. Smoking dope was never on my agenda. The looks on the faces of the customs officials, however, told me that all was not well and that I was in hot water.

I protested my innocence and insisted the bag did not belong to me but this claim was disregarded. The held me for several hours under interrogation in a small airless airport room before stamping my passport as an undesirable. I was banned from the country and, along with a confused and furious Karen, I was sent home on the next available plane.

We hadn't even left the airport. I was told later that the story hit the Norwegian newspapers and caused major embarrassment to Bryne FK and, no doubt, to the manager who had sought my signature on a contract. My excuse may have sounded feeble but it was the truth. It was an incident that was to return to haunt me many years later.

I returned, despondent, embarrassed and disappointed, to Moray. I played with Nairn County at the start of 1981 to bring up my fitness levels in the hope that an overseas club would come along. One of my team-mates was a teenager with undoubted talent, John McGinlay, who later went on to play for several teams in England before gaining a big-money move to Bolton Wanderers in the Premier League. He was also to win several caps as a striker for Scotland.

John and I were to form a deadly partnership for the little Highland League club, albeit only for a short spell. He was just 17 years old and his pre-match preparations were interesting, always consisting of him devouring a fish supper a couple of hours before kick-off, followed by a Mars bar and a Coke. But his diet never adversely affected his performance and even at such a young age you could recognise his natural goal-scoring instinct. John moved to New Zealand but our paths crossed again six years later in my first managerial post at Elgin City.

Not long into my spell with Nairn County I was contacted by an agent looking for young players to try their luck with a club in the Far East. At that time Hong Kong was a destination for many UK players who had either entered the twilight phase of their careers or others who didn't make it with professional clubs but could earn a very good tax-free living and enjoy a pleasant lifestyle in what was then a British colony.

I joined Hong Kong Rangers in February 1982. The club had been founded 24 years earlier by a Scot, Ian Petrie, who named the side after Glasgow Rangers, the team he had followed in his homeland. I was one of a number of Scottish players looking to keep their careers going a little longer by performing in a sub-standard football league. Previous Hong Kong Rangers players, like Willie Henderson, Jim Forrest and Billy Semple – formerly top dogs at Ibrox – had eventually ended their sporting lives there.

Six of us shared a flat; John Watson, later to return to Scotland to play for Dunfermline; Danny Rose, Tom Nolan, Ian Murdoch, Paul Rogers and me. The team had to include five players from Hong Kong with the remaining members of the squad being made up of Europeans, many of them Dutch.

We used to train at six in the morning before the sun was too hot. We lived hard and trained hard and sometimes went straight from whatever nightclub we had been drinking in to a training ground we often shared with the rats who hadn't made it back to the sewers before our arrival.

The wages were nothing to boast about but they were enough for us to live well and have a good time. Of course, for me, a good time included betting, and when someone in our group suggested we should take a trip to the gambling resort of Macau, I couldn't wait.

Off we went to this oriental Las Vegas, and I was as certain as I had always been before embarking on a binge of bets on the roulette wheel or the blackjack tables that I would return with a fistful of dollars.

Macau lies on the western side of the Pearl River Delta and its electrifying atmosphere got under my skin. This was my kind of place, with enough casinos to keep me occupied as long as I wanted. It boasted thriving tourism and textile industries, but it was gambling that was the big attraction for visitors and it was gambling that made it one of the richest cities in the world.

Lady luck was a good companion during that trip. That's why, when it was time to catch the last ferry back to Hong Kong, I had no intention of ditching her. But just as my compatriots gave up trying to persuade me to join them on the boat, her smile changed and my pig-headed attitude brought severe punishment.

Pretty soon after the departure of my friends I was clean out of cash, predictably losing every cent I had and, in those days before mobile phones, I had no way of contacting them to inform them of my predicament. I hadn't even enough coins for a phone box.

I panicked. I started to trawl the casinos, looking for any coins left in the hundreds of slot machines. With a monsoon having poured down incessantly for two days, flooding the streets of Macau, I waded, ankle deep, from casino to casino hoping to find that elusive cash so I could phone the flat in Hong Kong.

I was marooned. I needed to be rescued. Apart from not having slept for a couple of days, I was starving and my mind prompted me into believing I would be forgotten in this strange land and consigned to joining the down and outs already destroyed by Macau's gambling dens. This was the price I would pay for my stupidity and my ongoing need to bet until my pockets were empty.

When I grew tired and weary, my shoes squelching, my trousers dripping wet and my shirt stuck to my body, I tried to doss down on one of the many luxury couches the up-market gambling joints had scattered around their lobbies. Each time, though, I would fall foul of the security men whose job it was to keep out undesirables – suckers like me, hard-luck stories who had lost all their money and just wanted somewhere to lay their heads in the middle of the night. But our company was no longer required. We were a spent force and, without money, surplus to needs. We were defeated bums.

The bouncers carried walking sticks and whacked you over the legs to prompt you to move on. I remember hobbling my way across a lobby after I had been battered with a stick across the shins – thrown out for trying to get a little shut-eye on a settee.

My day out with my friends turned into two nights of sleeping rough. Eventually I did find a coin in a slot machine and used it to call Paul Rogers at the flat. He took the next available hovercraft crossing and rescued me. It was a scary time in a strange land.

Imagine trying to convince yourself that this was how a professional sportsman should behave. For me, it was simply another silly and needless episode in my chaotic life, one that I would laugh off as just another adventure, another story to tell.

Still, it was fun, and we got to play football, too, albeit with and against players who wouldn't be given the time of day back in the UK. That became apparent when Celtic came to town.

We played them in an exhibition game on 7 March, 1982, when, because they had been knocked out of the Scottish Cup by Aberdeen the previous month, they had a free weekend and were over to participate in a mini-tournament. Jimmy Bone, a former Celtic and St Mirren player, was in the Hong Kong side which went down 5–0 to goals by Frank McGarvey, Tommy Burns – who hit two – Tom McAdam and Roy Aitken. Also in the Celtic team that day were Packy Bonner, Danny McGrain and Murdo MacLeod.

During my season in Hong Kong, I became aware that there were a few games where it was apparent that the indigenous Chinese players were not giving total commitment and inevitably we would lose. On the other hand the foreign legion, despite our penchant for good living, was trying as hard as it could to win games.

One day, a club official came into training and handed us each an envelope stuffed with Hong Kong dollars. It suddenly hit us that we had unwittingly been drawn into a match-fixing scam. We decided to keep quiet about it and just take the money without querying why we were receiving such 'bonuses'. It wasn't unusual for us to be paid late by the club, so we were extremely grateful for any additional cash, even a 'lose' bonus.

The entire Hong Kong experience was a bit of an adventure for a bunch of Scottish lads in their early 20s who had neither responsibilities nor worries. After a season I had had enough. It was an end-of-the-road place for footballers, which wouldn't have been so bad had I been earning decent wages. Even if I had, they would have gone to the casinos or the racecourse book-makers or the bars and nightclubs.

Sometimes, too, there were hairy moments which might have had serious consequences, like the night the gang ate in a cheap, family-run backstreet restaurant. It was a bustling, noisy place where we were the only non-Chinese customers. We looked very out of place, especially as, pretty inebriated, we made fools of ourselves with our unsuccessful attempts to use chopsticks. Fellow diners would stare and point and laugh but we were too busy drinking and eating and enjoying ourselves to be bothered.

At one stage I went to the toilet, a stinking, unhygienic hole of a place right next to what could laughingly be described as the kitchen. When I returned to my table there were no friends, just a group of Chinese people headed by the burly chef waving a machete in front of my face and shouting in broken English. 'You pay! You pay!'

I was dumbfounded. What was going on? I wondered. Where were my pals? Then it struck me – they had done a runner, leaving me with the bill to pay. The only problem was, I didn't have enough money to settle-up and so started to try to enter into some kind of idiotic dialogue with the mad chef, who was still screaming 'You pay!' and turning to his henchmen. They jabbed me in the chest with their fingers and ranted and raved as if they were lunatics.

My mind raced at a hundred miles an hour. The machete seemed to get closer as I considered my options. Who was I kidding? I had only one option. As I couldn't reason with them and we didn't understand each other, I recognised that, with my back to the open door of the premises, I was nearer to the exit than they were.

I swivelled round, took several long and fast strides to the door, and I was away, up the narrow, dark alleyway, racing past dozens of similar eating houses. The fat chef and his gang were in hot pursuit, he flashing his machete and they jabbering on in their local dialect. There was one word in English they did know, however. 'Bastard! Bastard!' I heard from somewhere behind me. I never looked back and, thanks to my fitness, I was soon out of sight and guessed I had left them huffing and puffing in the middle of some street.

Needless to say, the story brought great laughter when I relayed it to my so-called mates, who thought leaving me high and dry was a big joke.

I could live without machete-chases through the backstreets of Hong Kong. I was ready to head home to the relative calm of Moray.

10

Down under with the Doc

It was late 1982. I played some Highland League games for Peterhead and Buckie Thistle as a trialist. Then in 1983 I made contact with Tommy Docherty, my old boss at Old Trafford, who had moved to Australia to manage Sydney Olympic, a high-profile job with a club supported by the thousands of Greeks who had emigrated to Australia.

Docherty had gone there for a final pay-day, years after the scandal at Manchester United.

I wasn't interested in Doc's private life. Playing football in the southern hemisphere appealed to me and, after a few months back in Mosstodloch, I headed off once more on my travels.

Playing for Sydney Olympic was a part-time affair. I trained Monday, Wednesday and Friday evenings and had a job by day to satisfy the immigration authorities. My salary from football was around the equivalent of £300 a week and I worked as a labourer on a house-building site, although I would generally find a quiet corner and sleep for much of my shift. The owner of the development company was also a major sponsor of the football club.

By then, my relationship with Karen, still back in Scotland, had ended. I was given an apartment at Coogee beach, a popular place with expat Scots who had gone out there on the £10 assisted passage scheme between 1945 and 1972 which was part of an Australian government policy to increase the country's population. The 'Ten Pound Poms', they were called. Migrants from other countries, notably Italy, West Germany, Turkey and Greece, were also encouraged to find the promised land of Oz.

It wasn't long, however, till I met a girl, five years older than me, with whom I was to share an apartment. Jan Richardson was a vivacious woman who enjoyed life to the full and was very much part of Sydney's café society and champagne set.

Jan, the daughter of a famous Australian professional golfer, Sam Richardson, an Aussie PGA Champion twice in the 1930s, owned a fashionable boutique where the city's wealthy young women shopped.

Her company certainly helped make my stay in Oz a memorable one but, like Karen before her, our relationship fizzled out when I later moved away.

My relationship with Tommy Doc Down Under was more as a friend than it had been when I was with Manchester United. He was great fun but he became frustrated with how poorly the club was being run. He was less ruthless than he had been and he enjoyed lots of pranks and practical jokes, particularly at airports, where the mischievous side of him came out.

Our league required us to fly regularly to places like Melbourne, Brisbane and Adelaide. At the time, the National Soccer League was not keen to include a club from Western Australia because of logistical, geographical and financial concerns.

Our air travel would involve flying on a Saturday night and stay over and play on a Sunday – Australia's soccer day. I remember flying into Melbourne and, along with all the passengers on the plane, waiting for our baggage to come round on the carousel. As hundreds of unsuspecting travellers waited for their luggage, Docherty, lying flat and perfectly still and with his eyes closed and arms folded over his chest, emerged from the baggage area on the carousel to the screams and gasps of those hovering around who thought they were seeing a corpse. It brought the place down and the players almost died laughing at his antics.

Somehow, I couldn't imagine him coming up with such a stunt when he was at Manchester United.

He was so unpredictably funny and impulsive and on many occasions during training sessions he would suddenly decide he would take Mary out for dinner that evening.

'Steve,' he would command, 'you're babysitting tonight.'

We would jump into the pink VW Beetle I owned and drive back to his house in the suburbs where I would look after his two young daughters. The Doc had a great attitude to life and was always my favourite gaffer.

The Olympic fans were a volatile lot and they frequently made it clear that they hated my guts because I had replaced a Greek player who had been a big favourite of theirs. No matter what I did or how many goals I scored, I was never going to be good enough for them. The club was Greek-run and Greek-sponsored and, if the punters had had their way, it would have comprised only Greek players.

It was not unusual for the fans to throw rotten tomatoes at me as I left the pitch if they deemed that I hadn't played well. A winning result, on the other hand, would spark parties, drinking and eating, and the traditional smashing of plates. Pity help us if we lost, however. Accusations of throwing the game would come . . . and the tomatoes.

Strangely, I never had any more problems with the ankle that had caused my early exit from English football and there was never any bother from it for the remainder of my career.

It was in Australia that I became best mates with a guy called Ricky Herbert, a New Zealand international who later became his country's national coach. He was a more than useful centre-back who competed in the 1982 World Cup finals in Spain where he and his defensive team-mates were run ragged in a 4–0 defeat by Brazil. He used to talk about that and how Zico fired two goals that day, with Falcao and Serginho grabbing the others.

Ricky had also played against Scotland in the tournament, with the Scots winning 5–2 with goals from Kenny Dalglish, John Robertson, Steve Archibald and two from John Wark.

Interestingly, Ricky, a great student of Scottish football, could even recall the full Scotland line-up that day:

Alan Rough (Partick Thistle); Danny McGrain (Celtic), Alan Hansen (Liverpool), Allan Evans (Aston Villa), Frank Gray (Leeds United); Gordon Strachan (Aberdeen), Graeme Souness (Liverpool), John Wark (Ipswich), John Robertson (Nottingham Forest), Kenny Dalglish (Liverpool), Alan Brazil (Ipswich). The substitutes were Tottenham Hotspur's Archibald, and David Narey of Dundee United.

How many of those professionals would be kept out of the current Scotland squad?

Ricky and I grew close through our joint love of gambling and he introduced me to the trotting races in any one of the numerous racecourses in and around Sydney. We'd also go to the horse and greyhound races and bet all our wages away. Apart from losing, it was a tremendous life for young men and we enjoyed it to the full.

Being paid weekly helped as it meant I didn't have the scope to build up big debts. I would get my football club and my building site wages each Friday. So if, as normally happened, any money I had was delivered into the hands of the bookmakers within two or three days, I didn't have long to wait until payday.

It was probably better that I was drip-fed my salary in that way. I certainly never saw my gambling as a problem. I was a punter and that's what I chose to do with my money and I took the view that I was a young, single guy and that betting gave me a kick. What was wrong with that?

A typical evening would be training from 5 p.m. to 7 p.m. then off to the race track from 8 p.m. to 10 p.m. followed by several hours in the nightclubs. Next day it was work, or, in my case, sleep on the building site

I spent March to November, a full season, in Sydney and loved every minute of it, except for those spoilsports, the Olympic supporters. We had had a reasonable season but by the time September came round we knew the team wasn't going to win the league as was expected and we recognised that Docherty was under pressure from the owners. There was also the little local difficulty of having Sydney City as our rivals. They were managed by Eddie Thomson, once a top defender with Heart of Midlothian and Aberdeen, who eventually went on to enjoy a successful career as the manager of the Australian national side.

Tragically, Eddie died of Non-Hodgkins Lymphoma in 2003, a few days short of his 56th birthday. He was a good man and he tried to get me back to Australia after I had finished my spell in Japan, my next stopping point.

City had the edge over us that season and that didn't go down well in our part of town. It was as the season was in its later stages that I was approached by a well-known sportswriter in Sydney called Tom Anderson, who had been contacted by a German coach called Rudi Gutendorf, just appointed manager of the Japanese club, Yomiuri, later known as Verdy Kawasaki and now FC Tokyo Verdy.

'Can you find me a tall goal-scoring centre-forward?' Gutendorf asked Anderson.

This question was the springboard for yet another foreign adventure.

11

An Oriental opportunity

The Japan Soccer League, or the JSL as it was better known, was still struggling to establish itself among the sports lovers of the country. Surprisingly, baseball was the major spectator sport. The hiring of Rudi Gutendorf was seen as a way to inject some interest into football, especially if he could attract European players to Yomiuri, the club owned by the leading media group in Tokyo and based in the city's Kawasaki, Kanagawa prefecture.

Gutendorf was a flamboyant character and impressed me when, with Tommy Docherty's permission, I flew from Sydney to Tokyo to meet him to discuss terms.

I hadn't heard of him at the time, but he was quick to tell me that he was the coach who had signed Kevin Keegan for Hamburg in 1977, and that he had managed a host of teams from VfB Stuttgart and Schalke 04 in the Bundesliga to Cristal Lima in Peru and Valladolid, then in the second division of the Spanish leagues. In addition, he had coached a wide range of national sides: Chile, Trinidad and Botswana among many others. He also boasted that he had managed the Australian national team beaten 2–1 by England under Ron Greenwood at the Sydney Cricket Ground in May 1980. In short, this man was a soccer mercenary and had probably had more employers than any other coach in the world. That was because he sometimes only stayed weeks in a job.

Would I consider signing for Yomiuri on a £50,000-a-year package for two years? That included a £40,000 salary, a rent-free apartment and a car. Try and stop me, I told him. Within weeks, having secured my escape from Sydney Olympic, I was on my way. Along with a goalkeeper from the former Yugoslavia, a Croat named Vjeran Simunic, I would be the first European footballer to play in the JSL. Gutendorf told the media and, more importantly, the club's owners, that Yomiuri were headed for glory.

Pretty soon, with my height and physique proving immensely advantageous, I was banging in the goals and attracting a great deal of attention. I was asked to pose for photo-shoots. Television companies ran features about me on the local channels. I was even the face of the JSL in a poster campaign to bring in the crowds to see this 'new sport' which was set to take Japan by storm.

After only a few months in Tokyo coining in the money and enjoying the delights of the Fuchu racecourse, I met a girl with whom I was to form a close relationship. Her name was Hiromi and we met in a restaurant where she waited on my table and her femininity and girlish smile captivated me the first time I set eyes on her. Hiromi had no English and I had only a sprinkling of Japanese words I had picked up on the training ground. But I still made an attempt to ask if we could meet one night. Somehow, she and I both knew how to hurdle whatever barriers were between us and we did get together for dinner and then went to a karaoke bar where we sang and laughed and had fun, all with hardly a word exchanged, apart from 'no understand' from her and some shoulder shrugging from me.

It didn't take long for me to persuade her to move in with me and set up home in my flat in Kawasaki. Except there was a problem. She was married but estranged from her husband. She not only wondered how I would feel about that, she was also concerned that word might reach him that she was with another man. And not just any man – a foreign man.

The whole scenario, were it to have leaked out, would have painted her as a dishonourable woman in Japan in the 1980s. Her family, who lived in Osaka, would disown her and she would be cast out as a scarlet woman.

None of this, however, could distract us from our affair. We wanted to be with each other and therefore agreed that we would have to adopt a clandestine approach to love which meant that we would leave the apartment separately if we were going out on the town and even travel apart from each other on the train into the centre of the vast city before meeting in a bar or a restaurant. It was bizarre but necessary. Not least because I was concerned that someone might report me to my employer, who would not have taken kindly to one of their players co-habiting with a married Japanese woman.

Hiromi soon got to know my little ways. My little gambling ways that is, and my penchant for losing large sums of money. She worked hard, I was producing the best football of my career, earning a barrow-load of money, and life was good.

It was around that time that fixed-odds betting on football games in the UK arrived on the gambling scene and this appealed greatly to me. After all, I was knowledgeable about the game so thought it would be a dawdle.

Once in a while, when the fixtures allowed, I would fly home from Tokyo for a long weekend, say from Thursday to Tuesday, an idiotic undertaking in days when flights were longer and less direct.

Still, I was the big man from Moray, local boy made good, and I felt on top of the world telling my tales of the Orient to my pals in the Garmouth pub or in the bookies of Elgin.

When I arrived home I would do so with plenty of money to add to the cash I was sending to my brother Andy, my conduit for the fixed odd betting on games in England. If we had a big win, and there were some, we would up the stakes and go for an even bigger success.

From Japan I would contact Andy weekly with the bets I needed placed and the whole machine would go into overdrive.

If there were warnings that this was a crazy move I paid no heed to them. I was earning the money, I told myself, and it was nobody's business but mine what I did with it. And anyway, if things fell flat with the fixed odds, they would be picked up at the Fuchu races. Except it didn't work out like that. It never does with gamblers.

On the football pitch things were going well. We won the league championship and the two major cup competitions, the Emperor's Cup and the Super Cup. We also played in the prestigious Kirin Cup tournament, beating the Uruguayan national side 4–3. I produced an outstanding performance, capped by scoring two goals. It was arguably the highlight of my playing career.

The second season started well enough until we began to hear rumblings of discontent about Gutendorf. His brusque style and aggressive shouting of instructions to his players were not fully appreciated by the Japanese members of the squad, who saw it as confrontational and alien to their culture of good manners.

It was clear they weren't producing their best form for the coach and he was shown the door by his impatient bosses, unhappy that he could not match the first season's success. His departure heralded the arrival of a Brazilian coach, keen to recruit South Americans for Yomiuri. The writing was on the wall for me and my Croation colleague, Vjeran Simunic, but I saw this as an opportunity to negotiate a sizeable pay-off, one that would help me square my borrowings and return to Scotland with the beautiful Hiromi and enough cash to start a business.

I was summoned to the office of the club's chief executive who informed me that my services were no longer required but that my contract would be honoured. It amounted to approximately £30,000 and when I requested that it might be paid in cash, the official bowed and said: 'If that is your wish.'

With that kind of money, an absolute fortune, I could have

returned to Scotland and very easily have started my own business. After all, the average weekly salary in the UK then was £184, while a teacher was earning £214.

I was told, too, that I could have any of the luxury goods in my apartment – a state-of-the-art television set, the most up-to-date stereo equipment and other items, valued at about £5000. They would be shipped to whatever address I chose. The club could not have been more accommodating and within two or three days I returned to the chief executive's office to be handed a new leather briefcase containing Japanese Yen to the value of £30,000. A one-way ticket to the UK, he told me, would be made available as soon as I knew when I wished to return home. We shook hands, he thanked me for my contribution to Yomiuri and apologised at the way our relationship had ended. I was instructed that I should vacate the apartment within two weeks and hand in the keys to my car at the same time. It was all so civilised.

I was happy. After all, my earnings had allowed me to buy a flat in Aberdeen, and here I was with the kind of money that would enable me to be self-sufficient. I could open a hotel, a pub in Elgin or maybe even a nightclub.

I vividly recall the moment on my arrival back in my flat in Kawasaki, opening the briefcase and staring at the bank notes, all brand new and crisp. My pulse started racing. I could turn this £30,000 into £60,000 in double-quick time at Fuchu. After all, it would soon be Saturday and the regular weekend meet there. I couldn't get to the race track quickly enough. Some kind of sensible thinking entered my head and I took only a third of my pay-off – £10,000 – with the aim of doubling it on day one. If anyone had delusions of grandeur it was me.

I set off on my mission with the thought that if I did lose the £10,000 at least I would have plenty back at the flat. And so I started off with bets of about £500 rising to £1000, doubling up when I was losing. It was disastrous. There were eight races on the card and by the sixth I was in a sweat, having lost £6000. Never mind, I told myself, there are two more races to recoup my losses. It would all come good.

I was kidding myself and I was in a downward spiral. By the end of the day the £10,000 was gone. I met up with Hiromi later and we went out for a meal and to a karaoke bar and enjoyed ourselves, although much of my thinking that night centred on what lay ahead the following day when, as I believed in my heart, I would clean up at Fuchu. I was totally pre-occupied that night and Hiromi knew that. No matter how hard she tried to bring me back to the present, my mind was in the future. I was already in a dreamland where the lure of gambling was too great to ignore.

On day two I travelled to the track with the rest of the money. This was to be my big day. Larger bets followed and while I had never panicked as a gambler, I was gripped. Nothing else in the world existed. It was impossible for me to walk away.

Over those two days I won here and there but because the first day was a total loss, the second simply brought bigger bets in order to compensate. It was a suicide mission for a gambler, chasing losses from the previous day.

I got off to a bad start and while to the outside world I remained cool, inside I was churning with nerves and there was a volcano erupting in my head telling me to stick at it, it would be fine. A substantial win was just around the corner. I was running out of corners. My wins that day were rare. It didn't matter. I was in for the long haul. I would not be beaten.

Ask any gambler on a losing streak and they will claim they are cursed, that the gods are conspiring to beat them. Paranoia takes over.

The losing streak continued and I started to become desperate. Everything was becoming very irrational, rather like that day in the bookies in Edinburgh where I needed a 6/1 bet to come up in order to recoup the loss of Karen's £600 holiday fund.

Forget the form, I told myself at Fuchu, just go for the bigger odds. Instead of placing a £1000 bet on a 2/1 favourite, it was £1000 on 6/1 and 7/1 shots. By then, I was a lost cause.

At the end of that second day my state of mind was fractious. I was totally consumed with my predicament. I half-knew that I was en route to losing everything from that smart valise the club had given me to carry the money. I couldn't stop – and I didn't want to. My mind was completely lost in the insane hysteria of gambling.

In the Tokyo sunset, I had blown away my £30,000 nest egg, the equivalent of £150,000 today, and my dreams of a luxury life.

That night, hoping to blank out the day, I went out and drank myself into a stupor. What else was there to do?

There were no thoughts about weighing up possibilities or form, or introducing some rational thinking to my behaviour that weekend. All that went out of the window. I threw money at my problem and it would have been just as well had I tossed it all in the Tama River that acts as a border between Kawasaki and Tokyo. I was on my own. It was anti-social in the extreme. This wasn't about enjoying a day out at the races. This was about pressing the self-destruct button once more as desperation kicked in and frenzied gambling took over.

It was chronic, addictive, dangerous and mad, and I didn't see it. I had lost everything.

Within a week or so, I was on a flight back home with the ticket provided by the football club. It was a heartbreaking time because of my deep relationship with Hiromi and we made a pact that she would join me in the UK as soon as was feasible so we could start a new life together.

My attempts to call her, however, proved futile and while we did correspond in writing for a time, whatever we'd had disappeared into the ether and we never saw each other again. Sadly, I had lost once more.

I walked away with a suitcase containing some belongings and left behind not only a woman but a world which had promised so much but which, aided by me, had underlined my inadequacies and flaws, problems I continually refused to address. The delivery of the TV, stereo equipment and those other expensive goods from my flat never materialised. Japan became another scene for my fruitless search for the kind of love and peace of mind that would endure.

In my Gamblers Anonymous notes, written while I was in the Sporting Chance Clinic, this is how I remembered that awful, mad, two-day betting binge in Tokyo:

> I remember having the money in new, crispy Yen notes and immediately fantasised that I could go to the local racecourse and at least double the £30,000 I had, perhaps win much more. I could then head home and buy a hotel or a pub and look after my family and mates.
>
> I was on a fucking massive high and couldn't wait for that race meeting. I headed off full of hopes and dreams. By the last race of the day I had done a lot of damage to my wad and was in what I would call a complete gambling frenzy, sweating heavily, thinking madly and betting bigger and bigger sums of money with each passing loser
>
> Fucking bad day at the office, I thought, but I was not beaten and still had £20,000 of my pay-off. Tomorrow was another day and I'd fuckin' be back to beat those Japanese bookies.

My notes continued about meeting Hiromi and getting drunk:

> Sunday arrived and I marched to Fuchu; loss after fuckin' loss. A dark day. A fucking new record loss. Dark day. All £30,000 gone by the last race.
>
> I think I even lost my train fare and had to get Hiromi to come and rescue me. I felt in a mad place, talking inside and

outside, my head saying things like: 'You stupid fucking arse-hole. What the fuck am I going to do now? My life's fucking ruined. I've let my folks down again. Bang goes the hotel.'

I blanked out my gargantuan losses in a haze of beer and saki. Inwardly, I had a fucking earthquake in my head. I had been truly fucked by Fuchu.

12

Mandy enters my life

Back home on Scottish soil and trying to cope psychologically with the enormity of my foolishness in those final days in Japan, my attention turned once more to football and what to do next.

There were thoughts, too, of Hiromi and what she might be going through since our split. I missed her but I knew in my heart that it was a love affair that was bound to fail – not only because of the geographical issues but because, deep down, I cared for no one but myself and my addiction. Important matters like love and family, all those things that go hand-in-hand with living a normal life, did not register on the Richter scale of my existence.

With my affection for Hiromi having flickered out, I contacted members of the local media in the north-east of Scotland, eager to make Highland League clubs aware that I was again looking to join their ranks, at least until my next adventure came along. Pele was back in town – down but not out.

At the Garmouth Hotel, meanwhile, I would stand in the low-ceilinged bar and regale regulars with my tales of the Far East, the lavish lifestyle and of my glory at Yomiuri. I told anyone who would listen about how we had been successful in winning all the cup competitions and how I had been a star performer when I played the Uruguay national side, scoring two goals against them in the Kirin Cup competition. I was 27 and at the peak of my condition – though quite what my internal organs were like with all the booze that I had drunk over a long period, I did not know. I was feeling on top of the world again after a very short period of remorse over my massive losses at Fuchu and my lost love, Hiromi.

At the same, I recognised that I was at a crossroads in my life and was torn between settling in Moray and accepting an offer from Eddie Thomson to return to Australia with his team, Sydney City. I decided to stay for the time being, unaware that my world travels as a footballer had come to an end. Interestingly, Thomson was to take over as boss of Sydney Olympic, my former club, the following year.

On hearing I was back in business, several Highland League clubs approached me with offers at a time when the race for the championship was hotting up and set to be decided between Elgin City, Peterhead, Inverness Caledonian and Forres Mechanics, a club which, in its 100-year history, had never won the league.

Harry McFadden was their manager and, with around a dozen games remaining of the season, I was persuaded by him and a couple of thousand pounds in a brown envelope – which I couldn't wait to take to the bookies – that I could help the Can-Cans achieve the impossible: win the championship.

My time with Mechanics was to prove extremely fruitful for me and for them. It kick-started my career, albeit at a lower level, and I was very influential in helping them to the Highland League crown for the first time in their history and in their centenary year.

Along the way, I scored some important goals and my experience and guile helped them greatly in a memorable season for me and the club. And, given that I was on a bonus if we won the title, the incentive was there for me.

The championship race came down to the wire and the last game of the season was against Inverness Caley – a long time before they became Inverness Caledonian Thistle. It was a tense, nail-biting climax and I'm positive that the Forres fans couldn't believe their team was in this position. We won 2–0 and I remember scoring the second goal with a volley from a corner kick. It was in May and there were stories that, when the crowd roared at Mosset Park as the ball hit the back of the net, golfers on the local course thought they were hearing a jet at RAF Lossiemouth 14 miles away. The championship was in the bag.

That night, all the bars in the town were packed to capacity and everyone was in the mood after an unforgettable day and a night. It was, however, probably only partly remembered because of the sea of alcohol drunk in Forres.

I was, of course, part-time with the club. I had taken a job as a trainee manager at the newly opened Joanna's nightclub in Elgin. That's where I met Mandy Bissett, the stunning-looking girl who was to become my wife and the mother of my two daughters. I had no great wish to be a nightclub boss so treated the job, as usual, as a social appointment. The staff would gather most nights after hours and we would drink until three or four o'clock in the morning. My relationship with Mandy blossomed. She was 19 and I was 28.

I pottered away at Joanna's for a year or so, and at one time the company which owned the club and the local bingo hall sent me a missive that, as part of my job, I would call out the numbers for all the punters playing bingo every night. I told them to piss off. I was having too good a time running the nightclub. Anyway, my street credibility would have been damaged. My ego couldn't have handled being a bingo caller and I shuddered to think what my mates would have made of it.

I was happy to remain at Forres Mechanics for the following season as I was enjoying my game and felt comfortable with my team-mates. With my nightclub job forming part of my social life I enjoyed my role as part-time footballer and fully-fledged gambler. That's how I saw myself. And why not? Gambling was my principal pursuit in life. Add on football, drinking and womanising and my way of living was complete.

A tragic and horrific accident, however, was to put a stop to my soccer career, albeit temporarily. At the time though, I wondered if I would every play football again.

It was not uncommon for some of my group, whether we were out drinking in Fochabers or Elgin after a Saturday game, to take a taxi for the hour-and-a-half journey to Aberdeen, where we could gamble in one of the Granite City's casinos. It was a good, if frequently costly, way of bringing a Saturday night to a close.

The taxi would be hired late in the night, and in high spirits we would make our way south to catch the last two or three hours at the roulette wheel or on the blackjack tables. If we blew all our money, and we usually did, we would grab a mince pie from a nearby baker at four o'clock in the morning then hop on the early train to Inverness, hiding in the toilets to escape the ticket collector, and jump off at Elgin station.

It was on one of those fun-packed Saturday nights, on 27 September 1986, that everything went horribly wrong. After playing for Forres that day, I met up with my brother Andy, himself a Highland League player, and with Graham Bowie, a friend who played for Keith. Our rendezvous point was the Grant Arms pub in Fochabers.

Having sunk a few drinks and analysed the respective games in which we had played that day, we ordered a taxi to take us to Elgin. Our thinking was simple – more alcohol, different surroundings. Andy jumped into the front passenger seat while Graham and I slunk into the back seat of the Ford Cortina car, driven by Peter Gill from Mosstodloch.

We headed for Elgin but we had hardly left Fochabers when Andy, who was playing for Lossiemouth at the time, commanded that we take a short detour past our house in Mosstodloch, just a mile or so en route to Elgin. I cannot recall why he demanded the stop-over. Perhaps he wanted a change of clothing.

We waited outside my parents' home for a few minutes,

although given our drunken state and annoyance that Andy's unscheduled diversion was taking up valuable boozing time, it seemed like an eternity.

Eventually, my brother emerged from the house and announced he had changed his mind. He no longer wished to go on a night out with us.

'I can't be arsed,' he said. 'I'm going to give it a miss.'

We took off, neither Graham nor I having shown any desire to take up the vacant seat next to the driver, and we drove off into the night. Minutes later our laughter and chit-chat were brought to an abrupt and crushing halt. We were about a quarter of a mile outside Lhanbryde when we saw a car coming towards us and swaying from side to side, its headlights shining right into our vehicle.

It was like watching something unfolding in slow motion as the vehicle got closer and closer, its lights blinding us and then, crash, it hit us square-on at high speed. Peter was killed outright. Graham suffered a broken jaw and other facial injuries, and I was knocked out of the car and on to the side of the road.

I slipped in and out of consciousness and I vaguely remember ambulance personnel attending me at the side of the road as people from the village gathered to see what was happening.

There was a lot of blood and I thought I had lost my arm because of a lack of feeling in it. I had been sitting directly behind the empty front passenger seat where Andy had been and the car just crumpled from the front, killing poor Peter. Had he been there, Andy would also have died.

All the physical damage I sustained came down my left side, from the gash in my foot, to knee and hip injuries and a dislocated shoulder as well as cuts and bruises to my face and head. I remember being tended by someone before we were taken to Dr Gray's Hospital in Elgin. The following day, and for some time after, Graham and I were in traction and suffering severely from our injuries.

But we were lucky. We were to mend. Peter, who had moved with his wife, Agnes, to the area 12 years earlier and had stayed in Mosstodloch for a decade, had been driving his taxi for only two months, having previously worked as a fork lift driver at the Baxters food factory in Fochabers. He was the father of four children and had his life snuffed out that horrible night. I felt guilty about what happened and how it affected the lives of all the loved ones he left behind. It was a shattering and traumatic experience for them and, all these years on, I still feel for them. Of course, that whole sorry incident left us with the biggest and most profound of questions: what made Andy decide not to take that trip to Elgin that night? He will tell you today that he doesn't know the answer.

David Edward, the 17-year-old driver of the car which was on the wrong side of the road and which drove straight into us, was convicted of reckless driving. He was fined £1500 and banned for seven years at Elgin Sheriff Court. He, too, had been seriously hurt and was airlifted by a Sea King helicopter from RAF Lossiemouth from the scene of the accident to Aberdeen Royal Infirmary.

I did not play football again that season because of my injuries and then Elgin City came along in 1988 looking for a player-manager, a trend made popular by Graeme Souness and Kenny Dalglish, who had assumed that role at Rangers and Liverpool respectively.

It appealed to me. But then of course it did. I was skint, still drinking, still gambling and still believing that better times were ahead.

My work at Joanna's and the fun that went with it, not to say the inordinate amount of Harvey Wallbangers I consumed every night, continued. It was party time whenever I was on duty and my pals enjoyed the hospitality to the full, as did all the staff members and their friends.

But I knew I had to get out of there. The heavy drinking was becoming a daily habit. It was then that I started out as a care worker, a job I fell into through visiting a school my sister and her husband ran. It was a school for children with behavioural difficulties – Cranloch School, near Lhanbryde, once a primary school but now re-opened as an educational establishment aimed at helping the children there to become more socially included in society. My brother-in-law was the head teacher and my sister, Morag, taught there. It all started with me taking the boy pupils for football training. Some of the kids attending Cranloch were living in Andrew Thomson House, a residential home in Elgin. I needed a job at the time and there were openings for relief care workers. The job not only suited my personality, but also offered me a way in to a career as a social worker. I was 30 years old and the only thing I knew about was football. But I soon came to recognise that I had a talent, too, for working with adolescents. It became my forte in social work.

13

Early gravitas at Elgin

Elgin City had gone through a long trophy drought. Raising standards and seeking success were a major challenge and I felt more than ready to take it on.

Whatever qualities I brought to the job, they certainly worked. Rebuilding the squad was paramount if I were to begin to make a difference at Borough Briggs, City's neat little ground. As a schoolboy I had watched the team of the 1960s win the Highland League Championship. Could I bring back those heady days? I was confident I could.

I quickly appointed Mike Winton as my assistant. I had received glowing reports about his integrity and ability as a coach and, of course, I was aware that he had been a first-class player in the great Keith side of the 1970s. My mate Mike Hendry became my youth coach as I believed it vital to have good and trustworthy people around me. It was a philosophy that remained throughout my managerial career.

In my first term with the club I played up front and we finished the season high up the table and won the North of Scotland Cup, no mean feat considering the depths to which Elgin had sunk.

It was a good year. Mandy and I had been living together since she had swept me off my feet the previous year when she arrived at Joanna's for a job. I had owned a house in Elgin where we originally set up home, but with my gambling debts once more piling up, I had to sell up to clear them. We moved in 1988 to a council flat in the Kingsmills area of Elgin, not the nicest part of town, and, after the nightclub job bit the dust, I worked as a relief member of staff at the children's home while managing Elgin City part-time. By then – 20 April 1988, to be precise – Jessica, our beautiful baby girl, was born at Aberdeen Maternity Hospital. I spent two days in the Granite City during Mandy's stay, after which she was told her recovery would continue at the maternity unit at Spynie Hospital in Elgin. With a bit of persuasion, I was allowed in the ambulance with her and was dropped of at Mosstodloch before my wife and new baby daughter continued on their way. It was a special time in my life. I was with the woman of my dreams and together we had produced a wonderful baby. It was a great feeling to be a dad for the first time.

I was relishing football management and surprised at how easy and relaxed it made me feel. I loved organising and training the players and was proud to be leading the 'black and whites'. Indeed, it felt natural and comfortable and words like 'pressure' didn't enter my vocabulary.

I was also fortunate that during my time at Borough Briggs there was an abundance of local Elgin lads who were to become outstanding players for me.

Ian McArthur and Mike Teasdale, both of whom followed me in later years to Inverness, were perfect to manage. Big 'Chico' McHardy, Russell McKay, Neef McLennan, Davie Mone and the wayward, yet gifted, John Teasdale – the main core of my team – were all Elgin boys.

The second season – always a manager's best, having cleared out the dead wood among his players – was exceptional. We cleaned-up – racing to the championship with a record number of goals. We enjoyed a great Scottish Cup run and won the North of Scotland and Scottish Qualifying cups. The treble had been achieved. We had also beaten Scottish Football League side, Arbroath, in the Scottish Cup before going out of the competition to Brechin City. I had effected a spectacular revival in Elgin City's fortunes and that was to show in attendances as local fans, recognising my attacking philosophy and my desire to entertain, returned to the ground. I had an eye for spotting players and, if necessary, converting them from one position to another where they blossomed and did well for the team.

It was the club's first championship in 19 years. The giants of the Highland League were back. The town of Elgin once more had a team to be proud of and the future looked bright.

The players worked hard, both in their day jobs and in training and they also enjoyed a drink. Occasionally, I would glean gossip that certain players had been seen drinking on a Friday night and that I needed to discipline them. However, I tended to turn a blind eye to such indiscretions.

One night I had a team meeting at training and, being a bit of a hypocrite, I informed them there was a ban on drinking on the eve of games and stressed the importance of being fully prepared for match days.

A voice at the back suddenly piped up: 'If you think I'm stopping having a dram on a Friday night, you've got to be fuckin' joking. I've done it for eight years since leaving school and I'm not stopping now.'

I was taken aback for a few seconds as I looked towards the voice. It belonged to Billy Ferries, a dynamic little winger and match-winner. He had been tremendous for the team all season and was a big favourite with the fans. Should I make an example of him? This was an early test of my management skills and decision-making.

'Right, Billy. I want a word with you after training.' Should I transfer-list him? Drop him from the side? No chance!

I instructed Billy that in future he should keep the sort of information to himself and, since he lived in the Black Isle, what I couldn't see didn't count.

His face broke into a big grin and he continued to torment full backs and was our player of the year. I suppose that night I learnt that, particularly with part-time players, a manager had to be flexible and make allowances.

It was at Elgin City that I first teamed up with Graeme Bennett. He was already there as a defender, and one I didn't rate at first. Indeed, I was prepared to accept an offer of £500 for him from Brora Rangers but he persuaded me to give him the chance to prove that that would be a wrong decision. I threw down the gauntlet and Graeme, or Grassa as he's known, became an outstanding member of the side. He was an intelligent sweeper who, while being the slowest thing on two legs, was a great passer of the ball and could read the game as well as anyone I've encountered. Later, I was to take him to Inverness Caledonian Thistle, where he rose to become director of football once his playing days were over.

Grassa produced a classic one-liner early in my time at Elgin, when we had made heavy weather of beating one of the Highland League's lesser sides. He announced in the dressing room, in his distinct Inverness accent that: 'We were fuckin' shite, but they were fuckin' shiter.'

I have often used that sentence over the years and it has never failed to produce a laugh. It is hardly the kind of post-match assessment Arsene Wenger might use, but it aptly summed-up that game for me.

It was during Elgin's Scottish Cup replay against Brechin at Glebe Park – we had drawn with them in the first game at home – that we were down 3–0 at half-time and Grassa and I came off the bench with thoughts of rescuing the situation. Instead, we made it worse and we ended up losing 8–0.

Paul Ritchie, a player I later signed for Caley Thistle, was our chief tormentor that day, banging in four goals for Brechin. I never forgot him and 'Dream' as he was known, did a good stint for me during the promotion years at Inverness.

So, what do you say to a bunch of players who have just been savaged on the football pitch? My style was not to barrack them or point the finger of blame. Instead, when we entered the dressing room at the end, I started laughing, and so did everybody else. That game and the result were too embarrassing for words. Nothing would have been achieved by moping or moaning. The answer was to raise our spirits as quickly as we could. I ordered everybody to get showered and dressed and we headed for the nearest pub.

My second season at Elgin also brought in better crowds. We were heading for the championship, the first for 19 years. I had reawakened the giant and I was beginning to think management was easy.

I signed a young lad for Elgin who had been working in New Zealand. He had just returned to his home in Fort William when I got wind of his availability. John McGinlay and I had crossed paths when we were at Nairn County in the early 1980s. I saw then at close quarters how talented a striker he was. By Christmas that season he had scored 20 goals for me at Elgin. His finishing was devastating and I knew I had a potential star on my hands.

Ian McNeill, a well-known football man in England, originally from the north, was manager of Shrewsbury Town at the time and came in for John and we transferred him for a record £25,000. It was a great piece of business for Elgin City.

Ian's career in England spanned playing for Leicester City and Brighton and Hove Albion, to management – he was at Shrewsbury and Wigan and assistant at Chelsea for a while. He became a major talent spotter for a range of clubs including Millwall, Leeds United, Norwich City and Bolton Wanderers – a club to which he later took McGinlay for a fee of £750,000. John was a late developer but blossomed into a top class striker and won 14 caps for Scotland.

My two years at Elgin gave me early gravitas as a manager and my success was particularly pleasing because of the affection I had always had for the club. I had revived the club and, at least for many fans, I could walk on water.

At the end of my second season it was time to renegotiate my contract and, given my achievements, I asked for my salary to be doubled: from £40 to £80 a week. I took the view that I had earned it.

My request didn't go down well with the chairman and his committee who ran the club. In fact, they were pretty shocked. A delegation arrived at my flat one night for a pre-arranged meeting and they told me that, after careful deliberation and because there were stories of others clubs showing an interest in me, they had agreed I should be offered an increase . . . of £10 a week.

I was stunned by their meanness. I might have been prepared to accept £70 a week, I told them. Then, one committee member looked me in the eye and said: 'We're not budging. We'll give you £50 a week and you have 24 hours to make your mind up.'

'I don't need 24 hours,' I said. 'I won't even need 24 seconds. Fuck off.'

I was angry and I admit I took a strop. It was unlike me but I knew I was being short-changed.

It wasn't long after that meeting that there was a dinner for representatives of the Highland League in the Mansion House Hotel in Elgin in May 1990. I was the man of the moment in the Highland League and that night I bumped into Forbes Shand, the multi-millionaire boss of R.B. Farquhar, a company known worldwide for the design and manufacture of accommodation units for the offshore oil industry and for pre-fabricated pods for hotel and leisure groups and for student accommodation.

Forbes was there in his capacity as chairman of Huntly FC and we met by chance in the gents' toilet that night. He had heard of my unhappiness with the Elgin committee and was interested when I mentioned their derisory offer which, he agreed, was not good enough for a manager who had guided them to so many honours in such a short time.

'I think I'm worth £80 a week,' I told him.

'I can do better than that,' he announced as we washed our hands in neighbouring basins. 'I'll give you £90 to join Huntly as a player.'

I was delighted, even though I knew Forbes had not consulted with the Huntly manager, Joe Harper, once a prolific and much-loved striker at Aberdeen, Everton and Hibernian.

It was around that time that I had completed my 'A' coaching qualifications at the SFA school at Largs where those who were keen to enter coaching or management would gather each summer and go through the various theory and practical drills, not to say enjoy the delights of the Ayrshire town's pubs every night.

I was happy to accept the Huntly offer. But, in October 1990, after a few months of results not going as well as Forbes had wanted, Joe was history and I was installed as player-manager – although because of my back problems, my appearances on the pitch were rare. I often wonder if Joe thought that when I signed for his team the writing was on the wall for him as manager.

I never looked back and I would argue that I created one of the finest teams ever to grace the Highland League.

Around this time, I moved into another council home, which I bought, in my native village of Mosstodloch where Mandy, Jessica and I lived. Needless to say, the signing-on fee from Forbes Shand helped greatly with the purchase price.

14

Happy days at Huntly

I was still gambling too much, gambling all the time. Had it not been for Forbes Shand's understanding in helping me with 'advanced' payments at times, matters would have escalated more quickly than they did. I was extremely happy and it was during my time with Huntly that I studied for my social work qualifications at the Robert Gordon Institute of Technology – now Robert Gordon University.

And what success I had in charge of such a wonderful team. We qualified for the Scottish Cup in four successive seasons and had lucrative ties against Dumbarton, Airdrie, Heart of Midlothian and Dundee United.

In season 1992/93 we faced Cove Rangers in the Tennent's Highland League Cup final, ironically at Elgin's Borough Briggs ground. It was the first final in Highland League history to be settled by penalty kicks after the game ended 1–1 following extra-time. With both sides having hit four from the penalty spot, I made it 5–4 for Huntly and we watched and waited as Doug Baxter, a former player at Christie Park, took the last of Cove's penalty kicks. It was saved by our goalkeeper, John Gardiner. Huntly had won the League Cup for the first time in 41 years and we were euphoric.

Incredibly, just a few months later, again at Borough Briggs, more history was created, this time in the Qualifying Cup. Cove were 1–0 ahead with minutes remaining until our striker, Brian Thomson, levelled the score to force the game into extra-time. Cove retook the lead but Thomson equalised once more and it went to penalties. Cove's John Wilson missed his spot kick and Huntly had become Qualifying Cup holders for the first time in their history. It was as remarkable as it was coincidental that we had beaten the same opposition, at the same venue, and both times by penalty kicks.

But better was still to come. In 1993–94, I was to lead the club to its first Highland League Championship in 64 years, beating the Inverness sides, Caledonian and Thistle, who were about to merge, and Ross County, a club bound for the Scottish Football League. 'Pele' had arrived as a highly-regarded coach and I felt nothing could stop me from building on my embryonic management career.

We had won the Highland League Cup for the second year in succession earlier in the season by beating Fraserburgh 4–1 at Borough Briggs with two goals from Gary Whyte, and one each from Brian Thomson and Eddie Copland, a fantastic leader on the pitch and a player you would trust to battle hard in every single match. Here's a man you'd like in the trenches with you, I used to think.

Eddie spent 19 years at Huntly, which was indicative of how highly he was regarded by a succession of managers. I recall one occasion when he and I negotiated a new contract for him as we relieved ourselves at the side of a country road while journeying back from a game in Fort William.

The talks on a new deal started as we left the bus along with the other players. We were packed with the beer we had on board the team bus for the trip home, and lined up beside some trees overlooking a loch. Eddie stood next to me and, as we hadn't got round to discussing terms for him to remain at the club, I thought this was as good a time as any. By the time we were finished urinating on a tree, Eddie had agreed to stay at Huntly for three more years. It was yet another example of my unorthodox management style.

Among my successes with the 'black and golds' was a 2–0

Scottish Cup win over Dumbarton, then sitting on top of the Third Division. Because our victory was unexpected it generated media interest and, having booked in that night at the Dunblane Hydro Hotel, we embarked on a night of unbridled drinking. The session eventually came to a close at four o'clock the following afternoon, proving that Huntly's players and staff were also champions at drinking as well as at football. I had been invited on to an evening news television programme to take part in the draw for the next round of the competition and sat alongside one of my all-time heroes, Billy McNeill, the former Celtic and Scotland centre half and, of course, the man who led the Lisbon Lions to become the first British side to win the European Cup in 1967.

How did my TV appearance go? I haven't a clue. I was so drunk that everything just washed over me, although when I later teamed up with the Huntly party, they assured me I appeared perfectly normal. We also won the Aberdeenshire Cup but, despite being ahead against Ross County in the Qualifying Cup final, we were beaten 2–1 in extra-time. It was the closest Huntly has ever come to achieving the Grand Slam.

It was at Huntly that I practised an unusual method of determining the best group of players to use and what they each brought to the team. When we travelled to away games I would hand out pieces of paper to every squad member and invite them to list the team they would choose that day and to detail what they thought of others in the squad. Those notes were seen only by me, of course, but it offered me a real insight into the personal views they held on each other.

This was a little bit of sports psychology that I brought into play at various times throughout my managerial career. My mind games normally worked a treat with my teams. We claimed the league title the following year. Cove, our nearest rivals, were 17 points behind in second place. It was yet another success in such a short space of time and, I suppose, it was inevitable that something bigger would come along. At the end of that season it did, in the shape of Inverness Caledonian Thistle, the new boys of the Scottish Football League.

Oh how hard it was to leave, though. Forbes Shand was the best chairman I ever worked for and he remained a great friend long after I left Christie Park. He never interfered. He believed in me and he made resources available to build what was, in Highland League terms, a hugely talented side. One of his qualities was that, like me, he never forgot his roots. Forbes is from a tiny place called Rhynie, in Aberdeenshire, and he retained the values with which he grew up. He never boasted nor showed any sign of ostentation, despite his enormous wealth. He, too, liked the fun aspect of being with a football club. Our team bus, for example, was always a party on wheels. If we played at Inverness, then on the way back to Huntly we would stop at pubs in Nairn, Elgin and Fochabers. There would be card games going on and massive carry-outs for the journey.

Forbes took the view that investment would bring success and that was what happened as we enjoyed good runs in the Scottish Cup and the financial rewards they brought – which were, in turn, ploughed back into the playing side. It was that kind of thinking that made Huntly the top club in the league for five years. Doug Rougvie, the former Aberdeen defender and part of the great Dons side that won the European Cup-Winners' Cup by beating Real Madrid in Gothenburg in 1983, took over the management reins and continued on the road I had set out with the players I had taken to the club.

There was no doubt that my management style caused surprise, some might even say shock, among some of my players. Dave McGinlay, dubbed 'son of Pele' because he was one of my favourites, would drive from his home in Fort William and collect me in his Vauxhall Astra, a black one as I remember, from Mosstodloch en route to home games in Huntly, a half hour's drive away.

Dave's initial concerns that I was never ready to go eventually evaporated and he came to learn that my approach to football matches was, well, different. Often he would arrive at my house to find me still in my dressing gown, fixed-odds coupon on my lap and filling in my bets for the afternoon's games up and down the country. On one occasion when time was extremely tight, he was nervously trying to urge me on, looking at his watch and hinting that we should be on our way. It was about 1.30 p.m. – an hour and a half before kick-off – when I announced that I was going to have my bath.

'But . . . Should we not . . . It's half past . . .' He spluttered.

'Don't worry,' I tried to assure him, 'we've plenty of time.'

We didn't have plenty of time, of course, and during our journey south I would work out what my team would be and my tactics for the day and then try to ignore the looks on the faces of the players when I arrived in the dressing room with only half an hour to spare. My time-keeping as a manager was nothing short of disgraceful, so bad that I would often have to fine myself under the rules I had introduced.

As for my gambling, I saw it as a normal part of my life. It was an integral component of the lifestyle I had chosen. It was me. But it was getting me into knots.

Mandy was not averse to a good time and together we would sometimes go through to the casino in Aberdeen. I was still a social animal and people who knew me accepted me for that. 'That's Pele: like's a bet, likes a drink. Good fun and a good football man.' I played up to that image.

Forbes knew I gambled – God knows, I borrowed money often enough from him – but I don't think he was aware of the extent of my problem. When, years later, he learned I was in the Sporting Chance Clinic to sort myself out, he contacted me. 'Why didn't you come to me? I would have helped you.'

He didn't know I was so ill, so addicted. I kept a lot to myself, just as I had kept secret that incident when I was thirteen years old and the victim of an attempted murder by a boy five years my senior.

Chronic gambling was a trigger for my drinking rather than the other way round. I would drink heavily at the weekends to blot out the losses and the debts and the chaos in my life.

In 1990 I started borrowing more and taking out bank loans as I became buried under a mountain of debt.

When credit cards became more readily available to an unsuspecting public in the 1980s and 1990s, and anybody could get one, it was a black time for me. It was worse than that. It was a disaster. I went out of control. Huntly Football Club was the one part of my life that was working properly.

Willie Lawson was my assistant. He'd been there with Joe Harper and stayed on with me. He was a great right-hand man, a man you could trust. When things were going well, as they always seemed to be at Huntly, he would frequently tell me: 'Pele, I love you.' He told me he loved me more than my wife ever did.

Willie's favourite line was: 'Is this a British movie?' He trotted it out every time we won a trophy.

I wanted him with me as my assistant when I later became manager of Inverness Caledonian Thistle but, because of his job with an oil-related company and the fact that he lived in Aberdeen, more than 100 miles away, he felt he would not be able to do the role justice.

He did a wonderful job for me at Huntly and held the fort when I had to have an operation for a back problem, which kept me out of action for a month.

It was coming to the close of the season and we were scheduled to play two games in the north; one in Inverness on the Saturday, followed by a trip to Brora Rangers on the Monday night. The team was booked in to a hotel in Inverness for the weekend and, having just been discharged from hospital, albeit still on crutches, I headed for the Highland capital to join the squad – but with no intention of stepping on Willie's toes.

There were guys at Huntly I liked so much – Brian Thomson, Arthur Murphy, Gary Whyte, Doug Rougvie and John Gardiner among them – and I knew being with the lads over a weekend would be tremendous fun. I wasn't going to miss out on that. And anyway, having been in a hospital bed for some time, I hadn't had a drink in what seemed like ages.

Inevitably, after the match in Inverness, there was the almost obligatory booze-up and once more I took it too far. In the wee small hours I staggered off in the direction of my room, the number of which I had forgotten, while my key was somewhere other than in my possession.

As I limped along the passage, however, I noticed that one room door was slightly ajar. I gently pushed it open and entered the twin-bed room where two people were sleeping.

On one pillow I could see the red hair of the sleeper. On the other, the hair was dark.

Good, I thought, Colin and Kevin Walker, brothers from the team; one ginger-haired, the other with dark locks. I was safe. I furtively entered the bathroom, stripped naked and proceeded to empty my bowels, courtesy of the many pints of Guinness I had consumed that night. The bathroom was not a pleasant place to be immediately afterwards. I hastily used one of the toothbrushes there to clean my teeth before stepping into the bedroom and, with the snoring reaching a crescendo, quietly removed one of their blankets and a pillow and settled down on the floor between the beds. Bliss.

Come the morning, rubbing the sleep from my eyes, a shock awaited me. On one side, in bed, there was an old woman and on the other her elderly husband.

'Good morning,' the woman's voice greeted me cheerily as she sat upright and sipped tea.

'Oh my God . . . I am so sorry. I don't . . .'

'Och, you're all right son. It happens all the time in Glasgow. Would you like a cup of tea?'

This couple from Glasgow took the whole ridiculous scenario, like a scene from a sitcom, in their stride. I could have been a murderer, or a robber, or a rapist. They never even batted an eyelid and went on to tell me all about their weekend and how they were in Inverness as members of a bowling club and there for a match.

At breakfast, the word had spread, and footballers and bowlers, all tucking into their corn flakes and porridge had a good laugh at what they thought a hilarious incident. For me, it was another major embarrassment, one of many which were the result of drunken binges.

I was 34 years old and always felt part of the squad, one of the lads. Maybe it was because I started out as a player-manager. I drank with the players, I drank with the supporters. Even in my days at Caley I used to get blazing drunk in the town with pals, players and fans.

It was totally irresponsible and unprofessional. I couldn't conform to what was expected of the manager of a Scottish League club. I would say that the vast majority of players who worked with me prior to the Aberdeen phase of my career, which I will delve into later, would say they loved playing for me.

I had felt at home with Huntly FC, which had a welcoming, family atmosphere. I was managing my debts, thanks to being paid weekly, and success seemed to breed success.

My second daughter, Emily, arrived on the scene in 1992 and chose a Saturday – match day – to do so. Mandy had had complications during Jessica's birth four years earlier and she was scheduled to have Emily at Aberdeen Maternity Hospital, where specialists would be on hand should there be any difficulties.

On the Saturday morning, Mandy informed me she was feeling poorly and, despite my protestations that everything would be fine, she insisted that she needed to go to hospital in Aberdeen. I have to confess that my mind was more on our game against Deveronvale that afternoon but, under pressure from a rather distressed partner, we headed down the A96 towards the Granite City.

We had just passed through Keith and with 50 miles of our journey remaining and as much consoling as I could offer, she turned to me and announced: 'Something's wrong. This baby's on the way.'

I was sweating. What would happen if the baby came in the car? Where would I get medical help? This can't be happening! Those and numerous other pieces of rhetoric bobbled around in my brain.

It was when we had just gone past Huntly that Mandy's waters burst and so, like some kind of mad rally driver, I did a hasty three-point turn and drove at high speed towards Huntly Cottage Hospital – only to find the obstacle of a parked lorry blocking the road. My patience snapped after only a few seconds as Mandy squealed with pain and commanded that I get her to hospital as quickly as I could. With workmen going back and forth between their vehicles and a nearby building, I stepped out of the car.

'She's having a baby!'

The lorry was quickly moved and twenty minutes after we reached the hospital, Emily was born. A year later, in July1993, Mandy and I were married in St Lucia, a dream wedding that almost turned into a nightmare before we even left the UK.

I was feeling good about myself, having guided Huntly to the league title and graduated with my social work diploma from the Robert Gordon Institute of Technology. Mandy, Jessica, Emily and I had arranged to stay in the Granite City at the home of my brother, Andy, the night before we were scheduled to fly to Heathrow on the first stage of our journey to the West Indies. We were to meet up with Mandy's parents at Aberdeen airport in the morning.

Our overnight stay coincided with a night out for all the graduates from the social work course and while Mandy begged me not to join them for fear of it jeopardising our trip, I dug my heels in and headed off with my colleagues. My memory of that night is blurred to say the least and I didn't return to Andy's home until breakfast time, just as Mandy was loading our luggage into a taxi in preparation for the wedding trip – despite there being no groom on the horizon until the last minute.

'Where are you going?' I slurred in Mandy's direction.

'I pleaded with you not to go out last night,' she fumed. 'I knew this would happen. You didn't care if we were going to miss the flight. Everything is booked, so I'm going out to St Lucia with or without you.'

I knew enough to realise that unless we left straight away the flight, not to say the wedding, was in danger of falling through. Typically, once I had started drinking on that night out, there was no thought of calling time on my boozing, or that I might put our plans in jeopardy. I was selfish in the extreme, which underlined my inability to prioritise.

The flights, first to London then on to St Lucia, were pretty silent affairs, partly because I was feeling dreadfully ill after a night of non-stop drinking, but principally because my wife-to-be was in no mood for polite conversation. Mandy explained – several times – that, as there was only one flight a week from London to St Lucia and we had to be on the island for at least five days before the wedding to allow for legal documentation to be arranged, it was downright bloody irresponsible of me to behave in such a manner. She was, of course, absolutely right. We were married on 6 July 1993 in the most beautiful of settings and we were there for two sun-drenched weeks, although Mandy forever reminded me that I had been just five minutes from missing my own wedding.

By then, my new bride knew the extent of my gambling and drinking waywardness. In the early days of our relationship she did some modelling in Edinburgh and lived in her uncle's flat in Easter Road. I visited her there one weekend and on the

Saturday I announced I was going round to the local shop for a newspaper. What I really needed was to find a betting shop and I didn't reappear for more than three hours.

I made up a story of someone having collapsed at the shop. I had gone to their aid and even travelled to the hospital in an ambulance with the patient. That day had nothing to do with a visit to a newsagents but I must admit that I even impressed myself with my story of being the Good Samaritan.

It was that same year that one of my best friends, Franny Slater, died of leukaemia. He was just 36 years old and it hit me very hard. Franny had done well for himself. He'd been to university and then went off to Africa, where he worked as a cartographer.

We played Cove Rangers in a cup final on the day of his funeral and I was determined to beat them and dedicate the victory to his memory. Franny was a lovely man with a warm, friendly nature and it seemed so unfair to have him taken from us and from his family at such a young age. Franny is buried near my father and my brother, Neil, at Bellie Cemetery. I visit his grave from time to time to pay my respects to a man with whom I shared many good times, growing up through Milne's High School. He was a very popular man and much-loved by family and friends.

While at Huntly I was given a gleaming sponsored car, a white Ford Sierra, as a reward for doing so well for the club. I remember the day of one game when I hadn't had time to make my usual trip to the bookies to place my fixed-odds coupon. I was in the dressing room when it occurred to me, so I turned to a young player, Stuart Mitchell, handed him the keys of the vehicle and issued the instruction: 'You're not playing today. Here are my car keys and here's my coupon. Put this on at the bookies in the town.' I gave him £100 for the bet and sent him off.

Stuart must have felt great in the new car because, instead of returning to see his team-mates in action, he decided to take the Sierra for a spin. At half-time, two policemen turned up in the dressing room area and asked to see me. They informed me that my car had been written off in Huntly a short time earlier. Stuart had crashed into a lamppost and wrecked my week-old vehicle.

Bloody hell, I thought, I'm in the middle of an important football match. I wasn't interested in the car and once I established that Stuart was uninjured – a surprise, given the speed at which he had been travelling and the impact of the crash – I returned to my team talk. Mind you, I was quick to find out at full-time whether he had placed the all-important coupon with the bookmaker to ascertain if it had been a 'jackpot Saturday' – a term I coined for a team victory and a fixed-odds success on the same day.

That was the way things were at Huntly and pre-match and post-match conversations were more about who was punting on which teams than they were about tactics or technique. We all had fixed-odd coupons on or bets on horses, which highlighted what was a big betting culture among the players, and I was the worst of the gambling group. How else could you explain why I would be listening to the radio at half-time to hear the result of the Grand National?

For the big races I would have an earpiece plugged in to a radio so I could listen to the commentary on the races in the dugout while play was in progress. Either that or I would have a contact near the dugout to act as my runner to update me on how my horses were doing. This was something I carried through to my time at Inverness, where it became part of the remit of Tommy Cumming, our kit man.

What happened at Huntly was unique. From never having won the title they became the top team for many years in the Highland League. Forbes Shand was the architect of that.

My dad, by now much more interested in my football life, loved going to the Huntly games, probably as much for the social aspect of it as anything else, and he tried to persuade me to remain with the Aberdeenshire club when Caley Thistle, who had spent one season in Division Three under Sergei Baltacha, came in for me.

'But this is a chance in league football,' I told him. 'I could make my name and go on to bigger things.'

He advised me against the move. 'The grass isn't always greener on the other side. You should stay put.' My dad was firmly in the Huntly camp.

What to do! Caley Thistle were pressing me for an answer. So, I did what I thought was logical. I put it to the vote in the Garmouth Hotel bar at a regular Saturday night knees-up.

'This is where I decide on whether to stay at Huntly,' I announced through a drunken haze to my friends and fellow regulars at the pub, 'or go to Inverness Caledonian Thistle. Let's have a show of hands.'

That Saturday night, Robbo, Jimmy Smith, Chas, Ernie, Bill and many others, all boozed-up, were the decision-makers and the overwhelming vote was that I should take on the new challenge at Inverness.

My wise counsel had spoken, prompting a nonsensical toast from me with a pint of Guinness. A new chapter in my management path was about to begin.

That is how I took my first step into league management and I was given what seemed like an impossible target by the Caley Thistle chairman of the day, Dougie McGilivray – to take the club into the Scottish Premier League within 10 years. This was not bravado on his part. Dougie meant it and his enthusiasm rubbed off on me.

I waved goodbye to Highland League football, still dubbed the man with the Midas touch. My spells at Elgin City and Huntly had brought fourteen trophies and I took my teams to the Scottish Cup on all of the seven occasions available to me. I had an average of two trophies a season. Not a bad ratio.

15

Triumph over the Auld Enemy

Before taking up my new job at Inverness I was asked to manage a Highland League select against an England semi-professional side, billed as an FA XI, at St Albans. My selection was slightly biased, with many of my players from Huntly recruited to the squad because of the fantastic job they had done for me. I wanted to be fair, however, and I selected players from other clubs like Brora Rangers and Lossiemouth and our large travelling party departed from Inverness airport on the Friday morning for the evening kick-off. The atmosphere among the group was happy – partly at the thought of facing the Auld Enemy, but also because this was seen as a chance for some serious end-of-season socialising.

The game was a wonderful occasion. From being 3–1 down and facing a vastly more physical England side with players earning ten times the wages of our lads, we ultimately triumphed 4–3. What we had in abundance was attacking flair and – a feature of all my great teams – skilful wingers. Marco De Barros and Stevie Gray, two hugely talented wide players, lined up along with their Huntly team mates, Martin Stewart, who scored the winning goal, Brian Thomson and Gary Whyte – three high-scoring strikers who ripped the English defence to shreds. I later signed Marco and Brian for Caley Thistle. But despite my efforts, I could never persuade Martin to follow them from Huntly. In my view he could have played at the highest level and perhaps gone on to represent his country. There is no doubt in my mind that he was the best 18-year-old I have ever seen. He was nicknamed 'local loon' by the players due to his contentment to remain at Huntly for his entire career and settle for his day job as a joiner with R.B. Farquhar in the Aberdeenshire town.

Martin was a gentleman who would simply shrug his shoulders when I would inform him that this club or that had offered £50,000 for him. 'I'm nae interested,' he would say. 'I like ma job and playin' for Huntly.' End of story.

The Highland League squad was: Hinchcliffe (Elgin), Pirie (Lossiemouth), Yeats and Rougvie (Huntly), Milne (Fraserburgh), D Whyte (Cove Rangers), Gray, Lennox, De Barros (Huntly), Gibson (Keith), Thomson, G Whyte, M Stewart (Huntly), I Stewart (Lossiemouth), Will (Keith), McKay (Brora).

Our scorers were: Thomson, Iain Stewart (penalty), Yeats and Martin Stewart.

After our victory over the English, one that will probably never be recorded again, spirits were sky-high as we set about our celebrations with the players, Highland League officials and Alan Scott, the ebullient Ulsterman and managing director of Aberdeen Journals, the newspaper group which sponsored us.

Alan, as those who know him will testify, is a social animal who loves to have a good time and, when given the chance, to hold court. He drank diet Pils lager with a tremendous enthusiasm and the more he consumed, the greater inclination he had to make speeches. At one stage, with an audience of extremely merry Highlanders at the hotel bar, he delivered a scathing attack on the English and concluded his diatribe with the announcement: 'It's a free bar for the next hour.'

Such generosity where free alcohol was involved spurred the group on to new levels of drinking and Alan was in his element, receiving a standing ovation in gratitude. By midnight, when the free drink was scheduled to cease, I took the initiative and made a speech of thanks to Alan and his company for their sponsorship and for the booze for which he had just paid. I then invited him to make another speech and, knowing his readiness to take centre stage, I was unsurprised to hear him again berate the English, wallow in the applause, and once more issue the call: 'The free bar is extended until 1 a.m.'

The party went into overdrive and as the clock ticked towards two o'clock in the morning, I encouraged our group to join in the song: 'One Alan Scott, there's only one Alan Scott . . .' Bingo.

'Enough,' he bellowed. 'Be quiet.' He banged his bottle on the table and again went into speech mode about injustices to the Scots and the Irish by England, a monologue that brought cheers from his audience and, more importantly, a further extension of the free bar on his tab. At 5 a.m. the barman waved his hands to signal we had drunk the place dry.

The following day some of the boys went off with the officials to see the FA Cup final while others joined me on a day out around the bars of St Albans.

That Saturday night at 11 p.m. those still standing were offered the benefit of some advice I decided to dispense. I told them they could probably rely on a free drink from Mike Tremlett, the Highland League correspondent for the *Press & Journal*, the morning newspaper for the north and north-east of Scotland, and the main publication of Aberdeen Journals. Mike was never known to hide his light under a bushel and loved being around the players and a part of the action.

I invited Tremlett to join us, although I omitted to tell him that I had suggested to the players that they should sign for their drinks on his account. It was even funnier when he offered to buy a round and we refused to allow him to do so.

The following morning Mike asked to speak to me privately and stated that he was in deep trouble with his boss, Alan Scott, as his drinks bill amounted to £800, and he wondered if some of the players had been signing his name to their own orders at the bar.

'Eight hundred quid,' I exclaimed. 'I reckon Scotty or some of those Highland League committee members are taking the piss, Mike. That is way out of order. Me and the boys have just settled our bills.' He bought it.

The trip was a memorable one and a satisfying end to seven hugely enjoyable and successful seasons in the Highland League, winning trophies at Elgin City and Huntly. But the Garmouth pub vote had been taken. Despite my dad's reservations, I was heading for bigger things.

16

The McGilivray project

It was the summer of 1995. John Major was prime minister, Robson and Jerome had hit the high spots in the charts with 'Unchained Melody', *Braveheart* was breaking records at cinemas up and down the country and, by accepting my new chairman's challenge, I was ready for the biggest test of my short managerial career – to lead Inverness Caledonian Thistle all the way from Division Three and make them a Premier League club by 2005.

A compensation package for Huntly was worked out between McGilivray and Shand, with the latter keen to squeeze as much from the deal as possible. They agreed on £30,000 and everybody was happy.

The background to Caley Thistle was somewhat complex. On one side there were the visionaries who saw that, by uniting the three Inverness teams in the Highland League – Caledonian, Thistle and Clachnacuddin – there would be a realistic chance of winning a place as a member of the Scottish Football League. And then there were others, some might say traditionalists with old-fashioned ideas, who saw such unification as sacrilegious and vowed that they would never allow it to happen. When league bosses decided to admit two more clubs, the great concern was that, if the opportunity wasn't grasped and grasped quickly, clubs from the south would enter the league system without a fight.

In the end, Clach opted to remain in the Highland League and after an acrimonious and bitter fight between certain factions of the two remaining clubs over the new name of the club and what colours its players would wear, an agreement was reached.

Rather than Inverness United, which might have been a better name, and certainly less of a mouthful, Inverness Caledonian Thistle was born. To be honest, I had no interest in the politics of it all. I simply relished being the club's manager and couldn't wait to get started.

The previous manager, Sergei Baltacha, had left in May 1995, and, with McGilivray's challenging words still ringing in my ears, I was ready to take hold of the club's second season in league football. The Telford Street ground of the former Inverness Caledonian was our home and my first task was to find an assistant.

I had known Alex Caldwell for many years and admired what he had done at Lossiemouth as player-manager. Alex had been a defender with Dundee and St Johnstone, so there was no doubt that he knew the game and I was delighted when he accepted my invitation to be my Number 2.

Of course, those early days were all about building a squad to take us into Division Two within a couple of years. The McGilivray project allowed for two years in the third and second divisions while he gave me up to six years to move the club from the first to the SPL.

My reputation in the Highland League served me well. Many players wanted to be part of my Inverness revolution and, with Dougie's willingness to splash the cash, I was able to hand-pick the men I knew could win promotion within two seasons.

I started by recruiting Iain Stewart, a small but deadly striker with Lossiemouth who, the previous season, had scored a remarkable 40 goals. The clubs couldn't agree a fee, however. The affair went to a tribunal and Lossie were awarded £30,000. So began the assembly of my squad as I looked to build an attacking force as well as a steady defence.

Eyebrows were raised when, after just four games, I replaced the goalkeeper, Mark McRitchie, with Jim Calder, a veteran at 35 years old. It was one of the best moves I ever made and he remained an influential player for me in those difficult early days when we struggled against established league sides. This was the real deal for me. I was a football manager who knew he wouldn't last long if results were not forthcoming.

The acrimony between the supporters who hadn't wanted to see an Inverness merger rumbled on for years but at least I was seen as a neutral coming in as manager.

My only interest was putting together a team that would get us out of the third division.

Baltacha's squad didn't suit me. He had used around 27 players the previous season, so I had a great deal of sorting out to do and it meant a massive clearout.

I reflected back on the Highland League select side I had managed to victory over the non-league English side in St Albans. There was a theory that you couldn't win promotion with a squad of players recruited from the Highland League. I didn't accept that.

I had faith in the quality of the players I brought in, some of the best of them coming from the league I knew so well. It cost Caley money but McGilivray backed my judgement. As well as signing Iain Stewart for a record transfer fee, I bought Ian McArthur from Elgin City for £20,000. We were prepared to spend. Unfortunately, the other clubs knew that and bumped up their prices.

The Caley Thistle job was part-time but well paid. I was also working in a children's home in Forres at the time so, between both occupations, I was doing quite well financially, allowing me, of course, to pursue my favourite hobby, gambling.

The club's previous season, their first in Division Three, saw Caley Thistle finish mid-table. Baltacha's style of football was defensive and not to the liking of many of the fans. I was a rip-roaring success at Huntly by playing attacking football and winning championships and it seemed to me that I would be an obvious appointment for Inverness.

What lay ahead in my first, embryonic steps in league

management, however, brought me down to earth with a bang as one defeat followed another and I began to doubt whether I had what was required to take the club forward. Such doubts didn't last long.

Livingston whacked us in my first game in charge and there followed defeats from Alloa and Brechin, followed by a draw with Albion Rovers at Cliftonhill.

I soon found my feet, though, and felt good when we hit Alloa with a 5–0 defeat away from home, then went on a run of good results.

The Scottish Cup competition was to bring the biggest excitement of the 1995–96 season. We eliminated East Fife on penalty kicks following extra time, dumped Stenhousemuir out of the tournament, and, having won through to the last eight, hit the jackpot – we had a draw with Rangers. There was a problem though. Nothing about our Telford Street ground fitted the criteria to stage such a game. It would have to be played on neutral territory and the Scottish FA decided that Dundee United's Tannadice Park would be the venue.

If there had been a choice between facing Rangers in the Scottish Cup quarter-final and losing out on promotion, or winning promotion and being knocked out in the first round of the competition, I would have opted for the latter. Any manager would say the same. But I was conscious that the club had spent in excess of £100,000 that season in bringing me in and allowing me to recruit a swathe of new players. In many ways the ideal outcome from Tannadice would have been a draw followed by a replay at Ibrox.

The build-up to the game was a mixture of fun and excitement. At training, those in the squad who were Rangers fans would play the others, mostly followers of the other half of the Old Firm, Celtic. Indeed, we had the talented Charlie Christie, once on the Parkhead club's books, snapping and biting at the bluenoses every time there was a seven-a-side game.

The 300-mile round trip to Dundee did not put off 5,000 Caley Thistle supporters on 9 March 1996. The A9 between Inverness and Perth showed a heavy increase in traffic that day.

We stayed at the Dunblane Hydro on the Friday night, a night that developed into a big drinking session. Alongside me was Alex, my assistant, and Dr John MacAskill, the club physician from Fort William, who was medic to the Scotland under-21s. He was a great character and very much a social and sociable man.

Also there was my good friend and ally Tommy Cumming, then the kit man and later to become groundsman, and Ian Manning, the physiotherapist. I liked to have my backroom team around me and with all the players in bed, we assembled in the bar. Even the bus driver, Tony, was in the gang, along with one or two of the directors and Doug, the chairman. To say we had lots to drink would understate the level of alcohol consumption. The following morning, hours away from squaring up to the mighty Glasgow Rangers Football Club in the quarter-final of the Scottish Cup, I was very hungover.

After breakfast, having stopped our all-night session only shortly before, I called a meeting for Alex and I to run through our instructions for the game and how we would approach it. We stood facing the squad, a flip chart behind us and took our lead not so much from the Brian Clough–Peter Taylor partnership, nor the Alex Ferguson–Archie Knox pairing, but from Morcambe and Wise or Laurel and Hardy. We simply made a big joke of the whole occasion and drew silly images and cartoons on the flip chart as the room filled with laughter.

The serious preparation had been done and I felt it important to change the mood and relax the players with my schoolboy behaviour.

We took the view that this was a day to enjoy and celebrate. We did not pretend that we had a chance. What we wanted was a respectable result, to come away from the game without being on the receiving end of a thrashing. That morning, Alex and I were the worse for wear and our antics lightened the mood and put everybody in a good frame of mind.

I wanted them to feel at ease. Had I gone into detail about the talents and danger posed by the likes of Paul Gascoigne, Brian Laudrup and Ally McCoist, I would have sent my players into that game in a state of terror. My management style was about my own team's preparation, not about any worries regarding the opposition.

On the day of the game, the Rangers fans in my group were lining up at Tannadice for the autographs of their heroes, having their pictures taken with them and 'booking' the jersey of the one they wanted at the end of the 90 minutes. We were Third Division and they were champions with a spattering of world-class players in their side. It was a magical occasion, even though we might have acted like a village team against their idols. In the end, we gave them a good game and enjoyed ourselves to the full in front of 12,500 supporters.

Gascoigne's scoring prowess came to the fore that day and he struck twice – one in each half – adding to Laudrup's opener and ending our interest in the competition. A 3–0 defeat and a decent performance from my team were as much as we could have hoped for.

My worries over our league form continued and, if anything, it worsened after that cup-tie. In the 10 league matches after we had beaten Stenhousemuir in the Scottish Cup, we won a paltry 14 points from a possible 30. I knew we could be in serious trouble.

Ross County had beaten us 2–1 at Dingwall the week after the Rangers game and I was furious at the manner of the defeat as well as our poor performance, especially against our arch rivals. I ripped into the players, something that happened only a couple of times each season. My dressing-room rant meant the press had to wait a little longer than usual – 30 minutes – for my post-match comments

I remember my words to reporters that day: 'Basically, I've lost confidence in my team and realistically on current form we have no chance of promotion. The Inverness Caledonian Thistle players are the best paid in the Third Division and, quite simply, if they can't do the job, I'll get rid of them.'

This was from a manager who wasn't exactly leading by example. After all, the social side of Inverness, the town as well as the club, rated highly among my priorities. I would be the one to lead the players to the Caley Social Club after home games and I normally ended up drunk and hiring a taxi to take me home to Garmouth, more than 40 miles away. I had moved there in 1995 with Mandy and the girls, taking a house right next door to the Garmouth Hotel. Had there been a bookies on the other side I would have been in heaven.

Returning from away games we'd stop in at places like Bridge of Allan or Auchterarder and have a few beers and the obligatory carry-out on the bus, where I would be in among the players enjoying myself as much as they were.

For all my distractions, we still managed to finish in third place in Division Three, an encouraging start to my league career but not quite good enough. On a brighter note, Iain Stewart's 24 goals made him the league's top scorer, confirmation that I was right to persuade the club to part with £30,000 for his transfer.

Meanwhile, my gambling was confined mainly to fixed-odds betting on Saturdays because of the amount of time taken up with my day job as a social worker and managing the club. My drinking was a different matter and I seemed to spend any free time I had – and it wasn't much – in the pub with friends.

17

The Garmouth gang

When I moved permanently to Garmouth after accepting the Caley job in 1995, the village hotel became my second home. It had been mine and my dad's local for a long time before I moved there and sometimes we would cycle the three miles from Mosstodloch because we preferred the atmosphere and the company there.

But now this quaint, whitewashed building with its low ceilings and historic surroundings was just a stone's throw from my front door. I once stated, probably in a haze of Guinness, that I intended having a tunnel dug from my house to the bar.

There was no doubt that the amount of time I spent there was excessive. It was my escape from football management and from my gambling exploits, although such reasons were feeble and delusional. Football, gambling and golf were the three principal interests of all my mates who drank in there.

It was a place full of characters from all walks of life; from Chas the landlord and Jim the plumber, to Ernie the painter, offshore Mexican Mike, and Robbo from the council. There were never-ending stories and laughs and we all golfed together at the local course, an outstanding and picturesque test. Most of our leisure time, though, centred on gambling, either on TV races, fixed-odds football or on our regular card games, not to mention pool, darts and dominoes. If there was something, anything, to bet on, we were up for it.

On a Sunday afternoon, we would even have a bet on which pub regular would be next through the door and our booze-ups on those days would start at lunchtime when I would visit for my 'hair of the dog' having told Mandy and the kids I would be back in a couple of hours. 'I'm only having a few drinks . . . promise.'

Once I had had three or four pints of Guinness I was out of control and unable to bring a halt to my intake. That meant my 12.30 p.m. start would end at closing time. It was wrong and I knew it, but I chose drinking with my pub mates over being at home with Mandy, Jessica and Emily and accepting the responsibility of being a husband and father.

With Jim Smith, a local plumber, I had a regular cabaret act which comprised a load of nonsense, with Jim assuming the role of a cowboy and me an Arapaho Indian – or native American as you're supposed to call them in this age of political correctness. The more I drank, the crazier I became and other characters would be adopted, from a World War One soldier to an American gangster. I would announce these characters were me in a past life, and, as Arapaho Steve and Jim the cowboy, we could argue for hours about the Wild West, each of us taking on the voices of our alter egos. Another regular, Ranald, would join in as an Apache. Any visitors who entered the bar would see the Inverness Caley Thistle manager – and later the boss of Aberdeen – in a different light. Jim's wife, Kim, kept a note of those Sunday cabarets and in one year we did fifty performances. Mad Sundays, indeed.

Robbo and I had a regular hour-long get-together on Friday nights to debate the next day's fixed-odds menu. Forget the Caley Thistle game, my number one priority was to sort out my trebles and bankers for the coupon. We could name every horse racetrack in the UK and Ireland and I confess that, from the comparative comfort of a bookies, I have lost money at every single one over the years.

My brother Andy was quite a naïve gambler, and, in the pub one day, he reckoned he was set to be rich with a bet on the more than 70 fixtures. He proceeded to mark 1, 2 or X beside every fixture believing this would pay well. I told him if his £1 stake came up he would overtake the Sultan of Brunei as the richest man on the planet with the unlikely odds of 100,000,000,000–1. Poor 'Pep' was never allowed to forget his 70-match accumulator bet.

Then there was the card game, Chase the Ace, which became popular in the pub. All the regulars would join in and sometimes we would be there until six o'clock the following morning at weekends.

The Garmouth Gang would have annual jaunts to Perth Races, great occasions if you managed to remain sensible. On one of those days out I emerged £2000 wealthier, thanks to a tip from Paul Cherry, who played for me at Inverness. It didn't end too well, however, and after we trawled the Perth pubs that night, I jumped into a taxi to go to our hotel. It was only when I arrived inside that I realised I had left my jacket containing my winnings in the back seat. That £3 taxi ride actually cost me £2000.

Naturally, because I was so drunk on the night, I had no recollection of the kind of car in which I had been ferried. I just hope the driver enjoyed my ill-gotten gains and didn't throw the jacket away without first rummaging through the pockets.

Garmouth wasn't good for me because of my drinking and gambling, although it wouldn't have mattered where I had chosen to live at this period of my life as I was now under the control of my addictions and totally immersed in a dream world. In fact, some of my fondest memories of the village are of spending time with friends like the late Willie Grant, Mexican Mike and my many pals out on the golf course, playing for a sweep on a hot summer's day with a chilled beer.

The Garmouth Hotel pub was a special place. When I returned from Japan in 1986, I spent the best and closest years with my dad there, enjoying a pint together and playing dominoes. He was in his element and he had a good 15 years when he joined in the fun and was affectionately known as 'Mr Dominoes'.

My father was a lover of poetry and used to treat the customers to various renditions of Robert Burns and Omar Khayyam, his two favourite poets, whose works he learned to recite while at school. Bill Paterson: the bard of the Garmouth pub.

18

Mandy tires of the Manager of the Year

Moving into my second season at Inverness there was a need – if I was to keep to Doug McGilivray's timetable – to ensure that I had a squad capable of winning promotion to Division Two.

Mandy and I had been married only two years and already, because of my selfish and unforgivable behaviour, the cracks were beginning to show in our relationship. For me, the most important matter was how to manoeuvre the football club into a position where success would be achieved and, having embarked on a clear-out of playing staff, I turned my attention to identifying the players capable of meeting my demands.

Paul Cherry came in from St Johnstone, followed by Scott McLean, also from the Perth club. Barry Wilson, once at Ross County, our Highland rivals, but then with Raith Rovers, also arrived. His contribution to Caley Thistle over a long period after that was incalculable. There were others, of course, like Ross Tokely, a raw youngster I'd had at Huntly and a defender who blossomed into a fine Premier League player with the club.

There were times when I thought long and hard about addressing the issue of my gambling but such thoughts passed quickly. I enjoyed it too much to give it up, even though it was badly affecting my marriage.

Much of my activity on that score was kept from Mandy and I would always find ways of getting money – money she would never know about – to feed my habit. It meant I didn't encroach on the regular outgoings, like the mortgage payments and the telephone and utility bills. Such problems would all come later as my creditors started to get their teeth into me.

I remember going to the Cheltenham Festival in 1996 with the Garmouth Gang.

In essence, Cheltenham was a massive booze-up and I was chucked out of a pub or two for being out of line. I was never aggressive while under the influence, more of an arse who would annoy people and be a nuisance, some might say obnoxious.

All the while, the vicious circle of money lost to the book-makers, debts being called in and drinking to try and blot it all out was with me. Whenever it did impact on family finances, Mandy and I would discuss it and I would always pledge to stop my betting and drinking and sort myself out. Like everyone envel-oped by addiction, all my promises were empty and meaningless. The plain truth was that I couldn't stop. It was an impossibility, and I knew it. It was ingrained into my very being. I never wanted to give up gambling because it gave me a special excitement and a real buzz every single time I placed a bet.

The drinking progressed over the years until it reached a stage, later, when Mandy had had enough. By then I had put my stamp on the Inverness Caledonain Thistle team and that was a highlight. Coming third in the championship race the previous season primed us for meeting the two-years-to-promotion goal. I was desperate to prove that I was the best manager in the league and that, with the right players around me and properly motivated, I would hit our target.

Because I was so young – just 37 years old – I was still one of the guys and had exceptionally good relations with the players. That, I believed, was one of my strengths. Some people would see my reluctance to place barriers between myself and the players as unprofessional. What other manager would be up the back of the bus on the way home from an away game, drinking and playing cards with the team members?

I was dealing with a new and different pressure as the boss of a league team and I coped by drinking more, and while I had a reputation for being calm and unflappable, on the inside I was scared of failing and I did my best to mask the load I bore.

Season 1996–97 wasn't all plain sailing but the move from the run-down, ramshackle ground that was Telford Street, to the new Caledonian Stadium in the autumn of 1996, might have been something of a turning point. Beating Cowdenbeath in Fife on 19 October, the day before Telford Street's 117-year life was brought to a close with a friendly against a Highland League select, put us on top of the division.

Our new facility, in the shadow of the Kessock Bridge and just a long free-kick from the Moray Firth, opened on 6 November with a friendly against an Inverness Select. We won 6–2 and were on course for the Division Three title after a 1–1 draw in the first league game at the Caledonian Stadium three days later.

I remember Dougie McGilivray's smile that day. 'It's been great,' he beamed. 'I couldn't have asked for a better day. The stadium represents the dreams of everyone connected with the club. The only way is up.'

He was right. Securing the championship on 12 April with a 4–1 win against Albion Rovers at home was as good as it gets in management. By then, having earlier clinched promotion with-out having yet won the title, Dougie's drive and energy had again kicked in and he was adamant that the following season we would be full-time.

That suited me as, like the chairman, I wanted to build on our momentum. I had won three Manager of the Month awards that season and was named Manager of the Year. I was on top of the world. What I could not envisage was that there would be clashes of personalities with Dougie as he sought to interfere with my side of the business. And no manager worth his salt would put up with that.

Happy families in Mosstodloch, Mum, Dad, big brother and sister, Neil and Morag, while Andy is the baby of the Paterson group. I was about seven or eight-years-old in this photograph, taken around 1966.

The Manchester
United first-team
squad of 1979–80.
Back (left to right):
Kevin Moran, Jimmy
Nicholl, Gordon
McQueen, Paddy
Roche, Gary Bailey,
Steve Paterson,
Ashley Grimes, Joe
Jordan.
Middle (left–right):
Laurie Brown, Sammy
McIlroy, Andy Ritchie,
Mike Duxbury, Tommy
Connell, Jimmy
Greenhoff, Stewart
Houston, Tommy
Cavanagh, Dave
Sexton.
Front (left to right):
Mike Thomas, Tommy
Sloan, Lou Macari,
Martin Buchan, Ray
Wilkins, Steve
Coppell, Arthur
Albiston.

MANCHESTER UNITED F.C.

The Red Devils

Honours

FA CUP WINNERS
1909-1948-1963-1977
Finalists: 1957-1958-1976

FA CHARITY SHIELD WINNERS
1908-1911-1952-1956-1957-1965

FA YOUTH CUP WINNERS
1953-1954-1955-1956-1957-1964

WORLD CLUB CHAMPIONSHIP
FINALISTS
1968

Honours

EUROPEAN CUP
SEMI-FINALISTS
1957-1958-1966-1969
EUROPEAN CUP WINNERS
1968

FIRST DIVISION
LEAGUE CHAMPIONS
1908-1911-1952-1956-1957-1965-1967

SECOND DIVISION
LEAGUE CHAMPIONS
1936-1957

FOOTBALL LEAGUE
DIVISION 1 1979–80

© Manchester United F.C. Designed by Belman Associates Health

Top left. The hairstyle that prompted the nickname 'Big Bird' because my curly top looked like a bird's nest, according to Lou Macari. He later tweaked my moniker to 'Big Bud'.

Top right. From Mosstodloch to Manchester and early commercial opportunities by the club's marketing people.

Left. A collectors' item at Old Trafford ... at least for the youngsters who saved-up portrait cards of the Manchester United players.

Above. In action for Tokyo in the mid-1980s when I was recruited along with a Croatian goalkeeper as the Japan Soccer League's first-ever European players.

Right. Early success at Elgin City with my assistant Mike Winton.

Happy days at Huntly where we carried all before us. This team shot shows our trophy haul at the end of 1994–95, just before I left the club for Inverness Caley Thistle. *Huntly Express*

Celebrating our second Highland League championship win and warming up for a huge boozing session that night. *Huntly Express*

The Caley Thistle squad of 1998–99. (*Back*) Mike Newlands, Duncan Shearer, Jim Calder, Les Fridge, Martin Bavidge, Ross Tokely. (*Middle*) Steve Paterson, Scott Mclean, Charlie Christie, Paul Cherry, Wayne Addicoat, Paul Sheerin, Mike Teasdale, Alex Caldwell. (*Front*) Iain MacArthur, Barry Wilson, Mark McCulloch (captain), Gary Farquhar, Barry Robson, Richard Hastings. *Trevor Martin*

Steve Lennox, my captain at Huntly, joins me as we show off the Qualifying Cup, the league championship trophy and the Aberdeenshire Cup in 1995. *Huntly Express*

The end of my second season at Caley Thistle and a league championship success. Here I am with St Johnstone's Paul Sturrock, whose side won the first division title, as we are congratulated by Sir Alex Ferguson. *SNS Pix*

Former Home Secretary Dr John Reid poses for pictures with Doug McGilivray and I at the Caledonian Stadium. *Trevor Martin*

Mandy with our daughters Emily (centre) and Jessica in December 1996.
Aberdeen Journals Limited

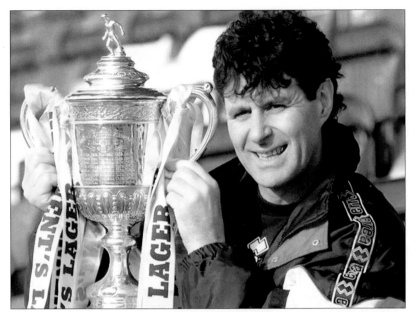

The obligatory press picture in preparation for the Scottish Cup-tie against Celtic at Parkhead. The sun shone and I knew we had a great chance to progress, despite the opposition. *Trevor Martin*

I was never noted for showing emotion during games but I was clearly ecstatic here after a 2-0 Caley Thistle win over Livingston. *Aberdeen Journals Limited*

The team bus from Celtic Park to Inverness was a happy place to be after we eclipsed Celtic in the Tennent's Scottish Cup. The Parkhead directors contributed to the joy by stocking our vehicle with beer. *SNS Pix*

This was how the *Sun* so brilliantly captured our momentous win over Celtic at Parkhead. The newspaper's headline, on 9 February 2000, made news, too, as media commentators around the UK applauded its inventiveness. *Scottish Sun*

It was hardly surprising that we were named the team of the round following our convincing triumph over Celtic and me and the players were only too happy to record the moment. *Trevor Martin*

Welcoming Ebbe Skovdahl to the Caledonian Stadium before a game against Aberdeen. Little did we know that I would soon be replacing him as manager at Pittodrie. *Trevor Martin*

The Inverness squad, pictured here in 2002–03 – continued to evolve but Duncan Shearer (front left) and I were soon to be heading for pastures new, a turbulent spell at Aberdeen. *Trevor Martin*

Ready for the SPL and set to take over the reins at Pittodrie. *Aberdeen Journals Limited*

Surveying the scene at Aberdeen and preparing for another training session as I tried to cope at a much bigger club. *Aberdeen Journals Limited*

Putting across my point to Duncan Shearer at Pittodrie as Oshor Williams looks on. *Derek Ironside*

The dreaded press conference three days after missing the game against Dundee. It was one of the most miserable experiences of my life as I sat before the media and admitted I had a drink problem. *Derek Ironside*

Tony Adams, the former Arsenal and England captain, visits the Sporting Chance Clinic, the superb facility he founded to help addicts like him and me. *Peter Kay, Sporting Chance Clinic*

19

Toughening up as a full-time boss

My debut year as a full-time football manager, 1997, also saw a marked increase in my drinking. Some players were moved on while others, preferring to stick to their day jobs and pursue their chosen careers, remained part-time. This brought about the unusual situation of having a mixture of full-time and part-time players and resulted in a kind of shift pattern for training sessions as we tried to accommodate everyone.

Richard Hastings, a local lad who had done well for me the previous season in defence, became my first full-timer and he would also turn out to be one of the club's longest-serving players. I had also brought in Les Fridge, a goalkeeper, and Vetle Andersen, a Norwegian defender, both of whom appeared for the club in an end-of-season friendly against Aberdeen. They had impressed me enough for me to offer them contracts.

Unfortunately, Andersen was to cause me problems. He was ordered off in a goalless draw against Brechin at the Caledonian Stadium after making some uncomplimentary comments to an assistant referee on his way to the dressing room at the end of what had been a frustrating afternoon for us, given our superiority. His remarks sparked a reaction from the referee who summoned us both to his room. I wasn't happy and my scowl indicated that in the clearest of ways. We were given the obligatory dressing down and afterwards I announced my unhappiness to the media over the incident. 'This kind of behaviour will not be tolerated at the club as long as I'm here.'

The following week I placed Andersen on the transfer list

after a training ground argument – effectively the straw that broke the camel's back. Alex Caldwell, my assistant, was from the old school of coaching and adopted a tough approach to the players when things were not going well. He used the 'run them' method as his way of sorting out difficulties, keeping the ball away from them in training and restricting sessions to running and physical exercises. Players detest that.

One day, a 'run them' day, produced a spat between Andersen and me after I had gathered the players on the training pitch to hear my views and to discuss the parlous state of our form. I demanded they focus more strongly on their task as we sat at the foot of the league table.

Following my pep talk, which brought no reaction, the players were instructed to pair up to begin a series of drills without the ball. It was then that I heard Andersen's voice. 'Oh sure,' he said sarcastically, 'this will make us a better team.'

My blood began to boil. He may have made a fair point but I knew I couldn't ignore it. He was undermining my authority and not only had I to take action but I had to be seen to be doing so. I remembered one piece of advice I'd been given about management: if you don't get rid of the troublemakers, they'll get rid of you. I pulled him aside. 'We're all in this together,' I seethed, 'and we don't need anyone pulling in the other direction. Now, fuck off back to the stadium and I'll speak to you later.'

He was shell-shocked and jogged the two miles back to base where, a couple of hours later, I told him he was finished at the club and that he had paid dearly for his comment. He stood there and wept. Vetle might have been a good defender but his influence on the others was detrimental to my efforts to lift them from the gloom hanging over us at that time. It was worth sacrificing his talent as I feared his attitude might have permeated through the squad.

He returned to Norway at the end of the season and I never

heard of him again. The incident sent out a message to the other players that this was about their livelihoods and about mine as well and that, if I needed to be ruthless, I would.

Sacking Vetle was out of character for me. I was generally mild-mannered and pretty much a soft touch when it came to disciplinary matters and fining players, though one, Scott McLean, gave me more than enough trouble.

I had signed him from St Johnstone, where Paul Sturrock, their manager, had described him as having good ability but the worst professional he'd encountered. Scott, nicknamed 'Trigger' after the hapless character in the TV comedy series *Only Fools and Horses*, shared a flat in Inverness with a group of other young players. I couldn't help liking him and, because of the daft-looking expression on his face, I found it difficult to become angry with him when I had occasion to reprimand him.

Sturrock was right about him: he did possess ability and he was strong when he needed to hold up the ball and link with other players. He also had a good ratio of goals-to-games during his time at Inverness.

He was, however, off his trolley and, because he was in-variably up to mischief, he was a frequent visitor to my office. One time he accepted a bet from some of his team-mates that he wouldn't run naked around the pitch after training one day. The £20 stake was too much for him to turn down and off he went, keen to win the money.

What he didn't know was that club officials were having an important conference in one of the lounges overlooking the pitch that day and when he appeared at the end of the tunnel, wearing only trainers and proceeded on his lap of honour, egged-on by hysterical colleagues, the spectators in business suits looked on in disbelief.

The chairman failed to see the funny side and came raging into my office. 'It's fucking Trigger again,' he screamed. 'You need to sort him out. There are people having lunch upstairs and he's running around bollock naked.'

It was hard to keep a straight face while lecturing 'Trigger' later, and I couldn't stop laughing once I had delivered my reprimand. He had the kind of look on his face that made it impossible for anyone around him not to smile.

Another time, I was told that he performed regularly in a bar which held karaoke competitions and Scott would sing Elvis songs, ripping off his top and giving his all to the audience in the town centre nightspot. Such priceless moments were witnessed by players, skulking in the shadows to see his deadly serious impersonations of 'The King'.

What a lad! Always late for training or spotted out drinking at the wrong time. Nonetheless, he was a key striker for us and a major contributer in helping us win promotion to Division One. Scott was like many 'bad' lads I had under my charge as a manager. I usually warmed to them and found it hard to enforce discipline on them. How could I when I was so undisciplined myself?

Although losing the plot with players was rare for me, it did happen more often when I was at Aberdeen, where results were consistently poor. My usual response to a bad result was not to go overboard with a rant but to emphasise the importance of rectifying matters in the next game. When I did launch into criticism of one of my teams, I would give them the usual Blarney: 'You're a disgrace. You've let the supporters down and you should look at yourselves in the mirror and ask if you've given your best.'

That, and all the other baloney managers have as their script at such times, was also how I played it, although I take the view that if you constantly go down this route, it can be totally ineffective and, as well as falling on deaf ears, it can prompt a lack of respect in you from the players. By using such tactics only sparingly, my players knew that when I would berate them, I had indeed blown a fuse and my feelings were real.

There were a couple of amusing moments at Inverness when the usual end to a post-match dressing-down would be for me to storm out of the dressing room, slamming the door behind me.

In my first season with the club, when we were still at Telford Street and I gave the team my first glimpse of my 'hairdryer' act, I ended up with egg on my face. I was unaware that one of the players, Mark McAllister, had locked the door from the inside and hidden the key. I finished my tirade and prepared to make my dramatic exit only to bang my head against the locked door in my haste to leave. The room erupted with laughter and I had to face the players, rubbing my sore head and calling them all a bunch of bastards.

There was another time, at the Caledonian Stadium where, having delivered my irate speech with both barrels, I went to slam the door for greater effect, only to catch my long, winter coat in it as it shut. I didn't re-enter the room but I could certainly hear the guffaws from inside.

Ross Tokely, whom I signed for Huntly and then for Inverness, and who was a favourite player of mine, once bore the brunt of my wrath during a cup-tie at Ayr United. At 1–0 up and playing well, we were on course for a great result when he was needlessly sent off and, as can happen, the match turned on his red card and we were thumped 5–1.

I was furious with Ross at half-time. 'You can get to fuck,' I ranted. 'I don't want you here. As far as I'm concerned you can walk back to Inverness.' Poor Rosco left the dressing room, still in his kit and actually made to make his way home before thinking how ridiculous that would be. Instead, he took refuge in the team bus. He sat there throughout the second half, frightened to return as he heard the roars that greeted every Ayr United goal.

My rants were rare and I certainly never held grudges against players. I believed that once the game was over and the talking completed, win or lose, you had to move on. In my case, that was usually to the nearest pub.

Whether it was being a full-time manager and all the pressure that that brought with it – after all, just about every manager gets the sack eventually – that determined my mood, I'm not sure. My gambling habit was constant and, while I didn't drink daily, I felt it almost essential to be in the frontline of socialising at the weekend. There was simply never enough alcohol to satisfy me.

I had a lot of belief in my ability but it was a very testing time for me, especially moving to full-time football. My livelihood depended on what happened on the pitch on a Saturday and I started drinking on Friday nights. At the start, it was a way of relaxing, but I was consuming an average of seven or eight pints of Guinness. In later seasons as my problems weighed heavily on me, once the pub closed I would order a carry-out and take a few lads back to the house to continue our session. I could easily have retreated to my home and had a couple of glasses of red wine but I always needed company.

Saturday was a big night for drinking. Almost single-handedly I boosted the profits of the Guinness brewing company. I couldn't even offer the excuse that I was either celebrating a win for my team or mourning a defeat. It had nothing to do with any of those matters. This was purely and simply about socialising and fun.

Then, there were the all-day sessions from lunchtime on Sunday till midnight. This went on for a couple of years when, over the course of a ten or twelve-hour period, I would down 20 pints of my favourite Irish thirst-quencher. Forget food. That was unimportant. Guinness was my nutrition.

On Mondays I would be so fuzzed-up from the booze that it took me until Wednesday to even begin to feel reasonably fine. Fortunately, our Monday training sessions didn't take place until the afternoons so I could try to sleep off my excesses in the mornings. That was all around the time that my success as a manager continued. And offers of bigger jobs with huge salaries and bonuses were just around the corner.

20

Guttered in Gourock

I may have had a laid-back exterior but internally, I bottled up a helluva lot and drinking was a release. Because I was earning more money at Caley, albeit a modest £40,000 compared with the carrots to be dangled in front of me soon after, my stakes at the bookies increased.

Inevitably, something had to give and the first house I bought in Garmouth was sold to pay off debts. Mandy, the kids and I moved into leased accommodation, again in Garmouth, but I had to borrow money from my father for the deposit and first month's rent.

My relationship with Dougie McGilivray became tense and fractured on occasion over what I saw as his meddling with team affairs – not so much a desire to have a say in who played, more on which players we should sign. For all that, I enjoyed working with him. He was a good chairman from my point of view but he may have felt under the cosh because of the financial difficulties the club was in.

Maybe Dougie had been a bit cavalier with funds. In any event, the finances of the club had later to be restructured and he was eventually ushered towards the exit. This was disappointing, given that it was his energy and vision that were largely responsible for hoisting Inverness Caledonian Thistle from obscurity to prominence in Scottish football.

He owned a thriving company called Weldex, an international crane hire company, whose offices were just round the corner from the new stadium which meant he almost lived at the club. I'd see his black Audi outside my office first thing in the morning, after training, or at night.

While he meant well, he began to irk me, especially when results weren't going well and he was always ready with suggestions for new signings he felt would improve the team. This would have been fine had it been occasional, but it became a daily occurrence. Worse than that; some days I would have three audiences with him each day – morning, noon and in the evening, if I had had a double training session. It was pretty constant: three new players to sign every day, sometimes a dozen in a week.

One day I cracked and we came to blows in my office, which was totally out of character for me. 'I can't fuckin' handle this any more, Dougie,' I shouted. 'You want to sign half the league. We'll have a squad the size of an American football team if you have your way. Fuckin' back off.'

He got the message and we soon made up.

There was one falling-out with Dougie which happened on the eve of an important match against Morton at their Cappielow ground in Greenock. We travelled down the night before the game and stayed in a hotel in Gourock. The atmosphere between the chairman and I at this period was rather icy. We had our evening meal in the hotel and instructions were passed to the players that there would be a curfew that they must adhere to and be in bed by 11 p.m. with breakfast the following morning between 8 a.m. and 9.a.m.

The row with Dougie had failed to achieve a compromise and I decided to unwind with a few beers.

Paul Sheerin and Barry Wilson sat for a while with me, Dr MacAskill and Duncan Shearer, recruited some time before from Aberdeen, mulling over the following day's game and talking football in general. In time, everyone filtered away to bed except for the Doc, himself a champion drinker, and me. We drank on and on and on into the night, consuming all manner of alcohol, including several bottles of champagne.

Then, as night turned into day, the players started arriving for breakfast, expressing surprise that the pair of us were still sitting at the bar at nine o'clock in the morning. Some of the senior players, realising their boss was as drunk as a skunk with only a few hours to kick-off, man-handled me to my room and into bed, hoping that in the short timescale leading up to the match, I might sober up, at least a little.

The pre-match talk then went ahead without me and they spruced me up as well as they could manage before helping me on to the team bus. This was all done without the knowledge of the chairman or the directors. I was placed along the back seat of the bus and slept all the way from Gourock to Greenock, although the three-mile trip was over far too soon for my liking.

There was concern that the chairman would see what a pathetic state I was in, but somehow Duncan Shearer and some of the senior lads in the squad kept me out of Dougie's way. Duncan made the excuse to the players that I had been upset by a disagreement I'd had with the chairman, hence my over-drinking. Some of them accepted that.

Barry Wilson took the pre-match warm-up. He called for a good result for the manager, who needed a lift after his rift with McGilivray.

I had been a bit under pressure because of a series of poor results and as I slunk into the dugout alongside Dr MacAskill to watch the match, my head thumped and I felt as if I'd been put through a wringer. Indeed, the club medicine man and I sat in silence for the duration, each praying for the full-time whistle and a sleep on the team bus back to Inverness.

In the end, we overwhelmed Morton 3–0 and the team performed as well as they had done for some time. It was a time to celebrate and while I was delighted and proud that the side had done their job, I hadn't the energy to display my emotions.

However, I had not lost my stupidity and when a reporter from Scottish Television came to our dressing room to request an interview with the manager, I had to be held back from participating. I shudder to think how that interview would have looked. Duncan stepped into the breach and did the honours for the television crew.

It was difficult with the part-timers. We had six of them and around 12 full-time playing staff and half a dozen youngsters on the Skillseekers programme. We would train Monday afternoons, Tuesday mornings or afternoons and then again at night and a double session on Thursday for the full-time lads. But players like Jim Calder, Paul Cherry and Iain McArthur, all on part-time contracts, were good enough to hold down places in the first team and contributed well. Davie Ross was another. He was a good player for me at that time and had a day job with his father's fish business in Kinlochbervie.

He would travel hundreds of miles a week for training and playing. He loved his football. For a Saturday game, he would rise at 5 a.m. and not be back home until nearly 24 hours later. All this without a moan or complaint, even when, despite his dedication, I would leave him out of the team.

'Daisy', as he was known, was a favourite of mine and I recall the difficulty I had telling him I was releasing him. He was a big, honest lad who always gave 100 per cent commitment in everything he did; playing, training and socialising. He would often bring boxes of fresh fish for the team on Saturdays and I hated it as a boss when I had to call time on such great types.

Over my long stint as a manager I was fortunate to work with some fantastic lads and the players knew when I had a soft spot for certain ones who were individually labelled 'Pele's son': Arthur Murphy and Eddie Copland at Huntly, and Barry Wilson, Barry Robson and Paul Sheerin at Caley Thistle all came into that category. My favourites were not always the best players but ones you could trust and rely on – Brian Thomson, Ian McArthur, Jim Calder, Paul Cherry; the list goes on.

That season, 1997–98, was all about finding our feet at a

higher level and it took us some time before we steadied the ship and sometimes I would feel keeping the two sets of players going was problematic. Being stuck at the foot of the table for a long period also preyed on my mind, as I had never experienced being in such a position. My resilience was tested to the full and I remember thinking that, now that all my eggs were in one basket in terms of full-time management, the ugly side of the beautiful game when chairmen usually give their managers a vote of confidence then sack them a week later, might just kick in were I to continue to fail to produce a winning side.

There was a Scottish Cup exit at Motherwell after a penalty shoot-out, but Duncan Shearer's arrival from Aberdeen in September 1997 was seen not only as a huge PR exercise but also as the signing of a proven goalscorer with experience at a high level. He had been at Chelsea, Huddersfield, Swindon Town and Blackburn Rovers, where he played just six games under Kenny Dalglish before moving to Pittodrie in 1992 for £500,000 – £300,000 less than the Ewood Park club had paid for him a few months earlier.

The Shearer signing was quickly followed by the capture of Barry Robson who was released by Rangers but was a player I believed could develop into a useful member of my squad. I didn't begin to think that he would turn out to be the star he later did with Dundee United, Celtic and Scotland. Although, had I had my way when I eventually moved to manage Aberdeen, he would have been with me at Pittodrie.

Injury and a lack of discipline had brought Robson's embryonic career with Rangers to an abrupt halt but my view was that, if he had at one time been good enough to be lured to Ibrox, he would surely have enough talent to do a job for Caley Thistle.

My intelligence from the football world told me he could be volatile and temperamental but I was never scared of tackling these issues with players and felt everybody deserved a chance, no matter their flaws, or what others perceived were their flaws. I could not be judgmental, considering the contents of my own locker.

I took the view that if you treated someone fairly and with respect then, generally speaking, you got the best out of them. That is something I discovered early in my social work career while dealing with difficult kids, and it worked for me in football. I've dealt with awkward and undisciplined characters many times and usually got the best out of them. It was one of my strengths as a manager.

For all my optimism, Robson had a poor start at Inverness and Alex Caldwell was keen to move him on. Barry's temperament was suspect and he frequently found himself in trouble with referees with his questionable on-field discipline. In short, he was a hot-head and sometimes I thought this big and strong left midfielder tried too hard.

The turning point with Barry was when we put him out on loan to Forfar Athletic because he wasn't cutting it with us. He needed to be playing weekly and to mature in certain aspects of his play and in his all-round mentality. I felt he was struggling and I don't mind admitting that he came close to being released.

When he returned from Forfar I saw a much-improved player with a strong work ethic and, just as importantly, a great attitude. From that point, his career took off as he channelled his energy and enthusiasm and aggression in the right direction.

But I do recall an occasion when he and two other players, who had been sharing a flat in Inverness vacated it to move to another apartment. Soon after they had gone, I was summoned to the place by the landlord and I feared the worst; a trashed and filthy abode for which I would, in some way, be held responsible in the eyes of the owner.

When I arrived, I was shocked as the landlord led me into the property and said: 'The place is a mess.'

He was right. Before they had left, his tenants had left the windows open and the flat now had new occupants – nesting pigeons. We went round all the rooms and the birds were everywhere, having made themselves at home, and the place was stinking. I had to make all the right noises before the landlord calmed down and the incident could be smoothed over. We had to hire a specialised cleaning service to deal with the problems the pigeons left behind.

Barry was one of my favourites at Inverness Caledonian Thistle. Even from those early days when he would fight in training or get sent off in games, there was something about him I liked. I had been warned not to touch him because of his indiscipline. He came with baggage and a reputation, but if you put your mind to it, you can find the good in everyone.

I found him a humorous guy and that spread throughout the dressing room. He had the best kind of attitude. You get the moaners at training but Barry couldn't get enough of work, although he despised the theory side of football, going over certain set pieces again and again, and just wanted to play games.

His enthusiasm was infectious. He just loved playing football with small sides and he would constantly bend my ear with: 'When are we having a game gaffer?' I would involve myself in those games on a Friday when I went out to 'nutmeg' Barry and when I succeeded I would laugh with delight while he would become angry and lunge at me as he sought retribution. For all that, his appetite for learning and diligence were relentless.

Barry made himself a better player and deserved his success at Dundee United followed by his big-money move to Celtic. My efforts to sign him for Aberdeen soon after I took over at Pittodrie proved futile because, despite his desire to play for me, Dundee United offered him double the wages the Dons were prepared to put on the table, as well as a longer deal. I could not compete.

21

New faces for a new division

With promotion to the First Division secured relatively comfortably at the end of the 1998–99 season, I was meeting the challenge set out by Dougie McGilivray – to reach the second top league within four years of taking on the manager's job. I was a hero to the fans and while I have never been comfortable with the fame game, I appreciated the congratulations of the supporters for what I had achieved. Could I keep it going? That was the question that often troubled me. And so was this one: how good could I have been without the baggage of gambling and excessive drinking sitting on my shoulders?

I tinkered with the squad as I assessed which of the players would be good enough to tackle football at this higher level and I signed a raw diamond of a centre-half from Forfar Athletic, a Dundee lad called Bobby Mann. What a stalwart he turned out to be for Caley Thistle and for me. He joined in February 1999 and by the summer of the following year, he was team captain.

Bobby was an enthusiastic defender and you could trust him to deliver nothing short of total commitment. There were others like him, notably Charlie Christie, in with the Caley Thistle bricks, so to speak, and as gifted a player as any around at the time. Not only did Charlie possess football talent in abundance, he was a tiger on the pitch and sometimes one with a short fuse. This manifested itself many times in training, so keen was he to win everything. Was there ever a more competitive footballer?

Charlie was a massively important figure for me and the club.

He could certainly have played at a much higher level but was a Caley Thistle man through and through.

Nonetheless, his competitive nature was sometimes a pain in the neck, a fact I discovered on my first day's training at the club. He and a player called Colin Mitchell, probably trying too hard to impress their new boss, became involved in a bout of fisticuffs. Given that neither would have caused Ricky Hatton to lose his beauty sleep, the incident was almost laughable and culminated in these two little guys scrapping away in what could have been billed the unofficial bantamweight boxing championship of the Highlands.

Charlie and Colin had the attitude of winners and I often wondered what would have happened to the former had he stuck it out at Celtic rather than turning his back on such a big club to return to his beloved Inverness.

My principal aim was to consolidate our place in the First Division. It was about survival and sending out a message to other teams in that league that we planned to stay around much longer than many of them believed we could.

My budget was not huge, however, and I had to call upon all my skills as a player-spotter to assemble a squad I believed could at least stabilise us. I brought in Stuart Golabek from Ross County and Kevin Byers from Raith Rovers. The Canadian internationalist, Davide Xausa, arrived from the Dutch side, Dordrecht 90, and Dennis Wyness, released by Aberdeen, was to become a major signing before going on to score more goals for Caley Thistle – 101 in three spells with the club – than anyone else. I had had Dennis on loan from the Dons in 1999 before I signed him on a permanent deal in January 2000.

There were difficult times, of course, as we tried to find our First Division feet and we did well enough to reach the final of the Bell's Challenge Cup at the Shyberry Excelsior Stadium in Airdrie, losing to Alloa Athletic in a penalty shoot-out.

That was in November 1999 and the following month

brought the departure from the club of Dougie McGilivray, keen to return to concentrating on his own business interests and to allow others to come in and sort out the perilous financial problems at the Caledonian Stadium. Dougie's dream of taking Caley Thistle to the Premier League within a decade was still very much on course and he was rightly proud of his achievement. David Sutherland, boss of the Tulloch house-building empire, was named chairman on 10 January 2000 and, recognising that on-field matters weren't going too well, he took the squad for an away day where we played golf at Royal Dornoch and enjoyed ourselves.

He clearly saw the wisdom of this initiative where everyone bonded and enjoyed a stress-free day. The idea certainly paid off and, with a fresh approach to football, our form picked up. It was just what we needed and with the new chairman left to concern himself with the club's escalating debt, I looked ahead to improvements on the pitch. I knew these would have to come as soon as possible as, the day before Sutherland took the reins of the club, we were drawn against Celtic in the third round of the Tennent's Scottish Cup. With pound signs flashing before his eyes and the chance to reduce the club's debt, he was smiling.

It was my fifth season at Inverness Caledonian Thistle and, like the players and the fans, not to say many of the citizens of the Highland capital, I was excited at the prospect of being involved in such a big game at Celtic Park.

It was to prove a remarkable cup-tie, the result of which reverberated round the world and left some of the biggest names in football in meltdown.

22

The night we went ballistic

The build-up to what was the biggest game in the brief history of Inverness Caledonian Thistle stuttered when the Scottish Cup third round tie against Celtic at Parkhead was dramatically postponed on Saturday, 29 January 2000.

How demoralising it was for me and my team as word came through while we were on the pitch inspecting the playing surface just 45 minutes before kick-off, that the game was postponed because part of the guttering of Celtic's new Lisbon Lions Stand had been ripped apart by high winds and deemed unsafe for supporters to occupy.

My thoughts turned to the 4,000 Caley fans who had headed south for the game and left disappointed and out of pocket. It was to have been my two hundredth game in charge of the team, and I was so looking forward to doing battle with a club I had admired since my schoolboy days.

The rearranged tie was set for the evening of Tuesday, 8 February. We had beaten Airdrie 4–1 the previous Saturday, with all my players emerging without injury. Mind you, it was a wonder none had bumps and bruises from our training sessions of five-a-side matches that pitted players who supported opposite sides of the Old Firm against each other. Bobby Mann, a bluenose through and through, was never averse to trying to hospitalise Mike Teasdale, who held a Celtic season ticket, while nobody needed reminding which colour Charlie Christie favoured. And for a diehard Rangers fan like Jim Calder, there was no crystal ball which could ever have foreseen him performing a seemingly impossible victory jig days later.

We arrived in Glasgow in time for lunch on the day of the game. A hotel had been booked in the city and the atmosphere on the bus journey from Inverness was a mixture of tension and excitement and expectation.

The post-lunch arrangements were that the players would go to bed for the afternoon in order to rest before the tie. A few, ones who had had jobs outside football either then or before they went full-time, joined me for a stroll through the streets of the city in search of a bookies, where we spent the remainder of the afternoon. They had never before gone to bed in the middle of the day and such a method of preparation was foreign to them. It was our way of relaxing, although, truthfully, I needed my fix. And what better way to pass the time than by donating a couple of hundred quid to Ladbrokes or William Hill, or whatever betting shop we settled on that day?

When, in the Parkhead away dressing room that night, I was informed of the Celtic line-up I was overcome with the belief that we were good enough to leave Glasgow with a victory. In my view, some of the Celtic players were simply not good enough to wear the green and white hoops and, of course, we had already been boosted by the fact that the great Henrik Larsson, one of my favourite players of all time, was already sidelined because of a broken leg.

I looked over their team: Gould; Boyd, Tebily, Mahe, Riseth; Healy, Blinker, Moravcik, Berkovic; Viduka, Burchill. This was no vintage Celtic side.

Bloody hell, I thought, we could beat this lot if every member of my team hits his best form. My philosophy throughout my managerial career had always been to try to go out to win games. Not for me the nonsense of looking to contain the opposition and hope for a break. Nor was I going to use a lone striker up front with a packed midfield to frustrate Celtic and aim to come out of the game having lost just a few, if any, goals. What would be the point of that?

Such tactics never made for an open game of football and certainly would not have pleased the supporters of either side. My take on the game is that you play not only to win but that you seek as many goals as you can. To some managers, this will appear naïve but this was the biggest night in the history of Caley Thistle. Why ruin it with negativity?

I chose this 4–4–2 formation: Calder; Tokely, Mann, Hastings, Golbek; Teasdale, Christie, McCulloch, Sheerin; Wilson, Wyness.

We wanted to take the game to Celtic. But hang on: what was I thinking about? After all, we were new boys to league football, with a team comprising a few part-timers. Then I remembered what we had already achieved and the more I glanced at the Celtic line-up, the greater my confidence grew. All I had to do was impart that to my squad.

I felt we were capable of scoring, no matter the opposition. If we could go in front then the Celtic fans would turn on their team. I gave the players licence to relax and to believe they could do it. 'You are playing at Celtic Park in front of a big crowd and on a good playing surface. It's a great occasion and one to be enjoyed. Have no fear.'

My feeling was that as well as the Celtic team not being particularly good, and with Larsson out, we had a real chance of causing a major upset. My optimism was underlined early in the game and as it progressed I turned to Alex Caldwell and said: 'You know something; we're looking the better team here.' Alex nodded his agreement.

At the same time, I was concerned our good start might be temporary. But when Barry Wilson's header hit the back of Jonathan Gould's net after just 16 minutes of play, I could hardly believe what I was seeing.

'Fucking hell,' I whispered to Alex as Celtic re-started the match, 'we've stirred the beast.' These words had hardly left my mouth when Mark Burchill raced up front to fire home their equaliser. Only a minute had passed since our goal, and Burchill's strike stunned me. Were we about to be on the end of a real hammering?

Thankfully, the players were unruffled by this set-back and we quickly regained our stride before Lubo Moravcik, as talented a player as ever wore the famous hoops of the Parkhead side, turned Bobby Mann's effort past his own goalkeeper in the twenty-fourth minute, allowing us to go in at half-time with a 2–1 lead.

I glanced at John Barnes, the Celtic manager, and Eric Black, his assistant, as they left their dugout for the dressing room. Like their players, their body language told the story of unease and trouble and for me that was as significant a sign as I needed that we were on track to win.

'We're leading this game on merit,' I stressed to my players at the interval. 'They're not liking this and their heads are down. There are clear problems in their camp. The fans are on their backs and that's the way we want it. We could be on the brink of something big.'

I believed every word of my half-time talk and, more importantly, so did my players. The haunted expressions on the faces of Barnes and Black told the story of their despair.

During that first-half, I could see that Mark Viduka, Celtic's powerful front man, wasn't in the mood and didn't like being clattered by Bobby Mann.

Despite this, I was extremely surprised when we re-started the game that he had been replaced by Ian Wright, the former Arsenal and England goalscorer who, through Barnes and Celtic's director of football, Kenny Dalglish, somehow ended up at Parkhead. He was a highly-paid, short-term replacement for the injured Larsson and a signing that proved disastrous for the Bhoys.

'Viduka must have picked up a knock during the first half,' I said to Alex Caldwell. He hadn't, and we later heard all the stories of what was supposed to have happened in the home dressing room during the break. Had he and Black clashed? Did the Celtic assistant boss really ask him if it was too cold for him out on the pitch? Was this the sarcastic remark that lit Viduka's fuse? Were blows exchanged?

All the passion from Celtic that night, if reports were to be believed, was kept for that half-time dressing-room soap opera. There was even one story that Viduka threw his boots in the bin and refused to come out for the second-half. Whatever went on, our opponents were rattled and we knew it.

Celtic, it must be remembered, had virtually handed the league title to Rangers by losing 3–2 to Hearts on the Saturday before we faced them and I knew their confidence and their will would be affected. What I didn't realise was that they were imploding.

I also recognised the disquiet among the Celtic supporters over what they saw as a rudderless and unhappy Parkhead ship where there was little harmony and a split in the dressing room. Indeed, Barnes would later admit that the capitulation to Hearts gave him concerns about team spirit and that by then he had lost the dressing room. I could have told him that at half-time in our tie against his bedraggled outfit.

Many of the fans were asking questions about Dalglish's role at the club. In fact, he wasn't even at our game. He was said to be golfing in Spain. So, all the signs were good for us and bad for Celtic and I was convinced we could capitalise on the disarray within Parkhead at the time.

This was a lightweight lot and I told my players that. On the night they went out and proved me right. The penalty goal from Paul Sheerin, a Celtic fan, just before an hour had been played, sealed our passage through to the next round of the Scottish Cup and everyone connected with Caley Thistle went wild with delight. We had cemented our place in Scottish football history, a fact blazed across the back pages of the newspapers the next morning when the *Sun* produced the now famous headline: SuperCaleyGoBallisticCelticAreAtrocious.

The unimaginable delight of that occasion was evident in the immediate post-match scenes with the players running to the Caley Thistle fans to accept the plaudits they so richly deserved. Needless to say, the bus journey back home for us was one of total euphoria and sheer, unbridled joy.

The Celtic directors stacked our bus with beer and we stopped at a hotel in Bridge of Allan to watch the highlights of the game on television. Those TV pictures confirmed what we all knew; this result was no fluke. We were streets ahead of Celtic with a side that contained several players who could have held their own at a higher level of football.

I did not sleep that night and, with the players, spent the following day at Inverness Golf Club, partly to relax and enjoy the triumph of the previous evening and partly to escape the media which, by then, was swarming all over the town. We talked through the game, kick by kick, throughout the day. Charlie Christie had run the Parkhead show and had the man-of-the-match champagne to display for his sparkling performance.

By the end of that day, we learned that John Barnes, Eric Black and coach Terry McDermott, had departed Celtic Park for good and we knew that Dalglish's position had also been jeopardised by the events of 8 February 2000. As we sat in the golf club quaffing as much alcohol as we could, Dalglish was en route to Glasgow from La Manga to accept responsibility for his part in a disastrous night for his team.

Unhappily for us, we were unlucky only to draw against Aberdeen in the next round before losing the replay 1–0 at Pittodrie. Our Scottish Cup dream was over for another year, but what a dream it had been.

23

Soiled boxers and a gay thumping

Now riding the crest of a wave because of the glorious win over Celtic in that famous Scottish Cup-tie, I recognised other clubs would be looking in my direction if and when a management job came up. But I was where I wanted to be, in the Highlands, and with a club with which I was at ease. In any case, would I wish to put myself into the goldfish bowl of a bigger set-up and have the media prying into my misdeeds?

My drinking had increased dramatically since becoming a full-time boss in 1997. There were embarrassing incidents, all linked with excessive drinking; like the night in Inverness when I found myself alone in the wee small hours after everyone who had been with me had scattered. The streets were empty and, after a night of Guinness drinking, I desperately needed to relieve myself. Where could I go?

My thoughts turned to the nearby Caledonian Hotel. I could use the toilet there, I thought. It was closed and in the end I staggered into a narrow alleyway deciding it would be my toilet. Too late; my bowels opened and I was a mess. I removed my filthy boxer shorts and tossed them into the River Ness which flows past the hotel, then flagged down a passing taxi.

'Listen mate,' I said, 'I've had an accident. Sorry about the smell. I'll pay an extra fifty quid. I need home.'

'Don't worry about it,' he reassured me. 'I have an old sheet in the boot and as long as you sit on that and we keep the windows open, it'll be all right.'

I gratefully jumped into the taxi, glad to be removed from this embarrassing scene. Here I was, the Caley Thistle manager, a hero earlier in the day and now an incontinent drunk being driven 50 miles down the Moray coast by a stranger. God only knows what was going through his mind.

I'm ashamed of that when I look back but that was how bad my drinking had become. Imagine being seen in such a boozed-up and ridiculous state or worse, that I might have been photographed throwing a pair of soiled boxer shorts into the River Ness.

There was also the time I was pub-hopping with colleagues and as usual I could never get enough drink. While it is common for social drinkers to have a couple of pints and then go home, I had always to stay until closing time, and even that wasn't enough. I became arrogant and obnoxious when I had been drinking and while I was never aggressive or violent, I was impudent and impertinent.

I recall coming across two gay men in the street. I said something cheeky and probably derogatory. Suddenly, wallop! One of them floored me with the shortest of punches, cutting my eye in the process. It was a thump and a sore face I deserved.

I readily mixed with fans and some would predictably see me as a target which would sometimes bring an exchange of views about my team, or my tactics, or the results we'd been having and end in a fight. Once, after a drinking session in the Red Lion pub in Fochabers. I emerged late one night and was jumped on by a couple of men and given a real kicking. My black eyes and bruising brought some interesting questions at the Caledonian Stadium the following day.

With my behavioural deterioration continuing and impacting on family life, Mandy once had to call the police when, in a crazed state after consuming an inordinate amount of whisky, I started punching holes in one of the walls in our house. I was never physically abusive to my wife but episodes like this were clear signs of my descent into alcoholism.

I referred to this and other appalling incidents in my work notes in the Sporting Chance Clinic:

I have driven while drunk a few times, crashing cars in the process. I even jumped off bridges into rivers for 'dares' or simply to show off. I've been cheeky to the wrong people in various towns, chatting up girls with boyfriends and being ejected from pubs and clubs. I have climbed high trees and swung about on them and walked on the parapet of bridges to gain attention. I stole a motorbike and fucked off without knowing how to control it.

I have required medical attention after being beaten up several times. I was drunk when I fell off my bike and almost severed my little finger. It was stitched back on. I once fell off my bike and lay unconscious with a head injury at the side of the road. I have fallen off bar stools on to my head and crashed cars several times, receiving various injuries including a dislocated shoulder and cuts and bruises. I fell into a ditch and was stuck there for three hours during winter, nearly freezing to death while trying to make my way home after a drinking spree.

Then there was a disgraceful act of unprofessionalism when, having been drinking into the early hours of Saturday morning, the day we were playing away to Falkirk, I awoke to realise I would never make it to the pick-up point for the team bus at Aviemore.

I phoned the club and informed somebody that I had changed my mind about my travel arrangements. I would drive directly to Brockville. I found a friend to be my chauffeur and I arrived at the ground half an hour before kick-off. It was obvious from the reaction of the players that they knew exactly why I was late. If they hadn't immediately cottoned-on, the stench from my breath would have told the tale. I mumbled a few short sentences of encouragement with the players laughing at my predicament. Nonetheless, I sent them out to win 2–1 and take top spot in the First Division.

But I was like a runaway train which was out of control and Mandy grew weary of my lifestyle and how it impacted on her and the girls.

It was soon after the victory at Celtic Park that Alex Caldwell moved on to become manager of Elgin City, a club I once managed in the Highland League and admitted to the SFL from season 2000–2001. Alex had done an excellent job at Inverness and I felt the club might have pushed the boat out to offer him a full-time contract that would have been worth him quitting his job as a transport manager.

Duncan Shearer, playing occasionally and coaching, too, became my assistant. He was the more vocal of the partnership and decidedly more animated than I ever was in the dugout. He was a good guy to have on board and we became close friends. I had been lucky through my managerial career to have good, trustworthy right-hand men and Duncan certainly fell into that category.

So, too, did John Docherty, formerly the manager of Inverness Caledonian in the Highland League but then out of football. I took him to the club as reserve coach and he subsequently saw a succession of managers come and go. John is one of those men every football club should have, and many do. They are the foundation stones of the organisations and players can go to them for guidance and advice. He was a mentor to them and sometimes a shoulder to cry on when they were troubled or had been barracked by the manager.

John is a man of genuine character and integrity and is held in the highest of esteem by all those fortunate enough to have come in contact with him; a benevolent uncle type to the players and a sounding board for the boss. Football needs men like John Docherty.

It would not be unrealistic to suggest that around this time

Mandy would have been a widow to my priorities . . . football, gambling and drinking. I wasn't there a lot of the time. I was a good football manager but a lousy husband and absentee father.

David Sutherland's chairmanship at the Caledonian Stadium brought with it the appointment of a director of football and we were in agreement that we needed someone who would be a link between the board and the playing side. I also insisted I needed someone I could trust. That man was Graeme Bennett, who had played for me at the club but who had moved on to Clachnacuddin, the sole Inverness side left in the Highland League.

We were still making good progress in a league full of excellent sides and we finished a creditable sixth in the league, having scored 80 goals, shared between 16 players. I was pleased with myself and with the contribution made by the squad, particularly the younger members, who looked comfortable in the Division One arena.

With progress came further changes. Inverness Caledonian Thistle's playing budget seemed to become tighter and I felt as though I was being asked to perform miracles with the resources available to me. However, my approach was simply to move ahead with the job and rely on my ability to spot and groom players.

The departure to Livingston of Barry Wilson and Mark McCulloch – we couldn't afford to retain them – gave us difficulties but did not dampen my determination to keep the club on track for the Premier League.

Charlie Christie was appointed player/coach with responsibility for the Skillseekers programme, aimed at bringing through youngsters. It was a role to which he warmed and an excellent move by the club.

Still, my gambling and drinking habits would not abate. We were in season 2001–2002 and my need to satisfy my craving for betting was all-consuming. What other football manager would have an aide close by the dugout with up-dates of results elsewhere? Was I really interested in those results to find out how they impacted on our league position, or how they might affect my fixed odds? I certainly tried to kid people on that it was for the former. Thank goodness for BBC Radio Scotland.

I can't remember having a Saturday without a good bet on the fixed odds and, even before my half-time lecture took place, someone would be sent to the nearest television set in whatever stadium we were playing to glean the latest news from other grounds. This task usually fell to Tommy Cumming, my loyal kit-man and trusted mate.

I wasn't even discreet when and where I placed my bets. After training I would go round to the bookmakers in the Ferry area of Inverness and place my coupon on the weekend's games or my lines on the horses. In Inverness, none of that was seen as bad. It was part of my make-up. Provided I was producing results, nobody bothered. That, at least, was how I saw it.

For me, managing a football team and having a reasonable measure of success was effortless. There was no struggle other than those with my demons. Looking back, I can see that I was also in the grip of complacency and that, as any football manager would agree, is professional suicide.

Instead of studying the game, new coaching methods and techniques and widening my horizons, I was too taken up with what mattered for me, my requirement to boost the profits of the bookmakers of Inverness and the north-east as well as help with the turnover of as many publicans as possible in the area.

Today, I look at someone like David Moyes, the manager of Everton, and wonder if I could have reached the upper echelons of the game, as he did. He and I did some coaching courses together and not only is he the nicest of men, he is obsessed with learning. Look at where it has taken him. He hauled Everton from the depths of the Premier League in England to playing in Europe and challenging for one of the top six spots, which is no

mean feat in the rarefied atmosphere near the summit of a hugely
competitive football league.

In all honesty, while I was enthusiastic and diligent when
going for my A coaching licence, I hit a time when I stopped
being motivated. I had no career plan. Moyes never reached the
heights as a player with Celtic and a host of provincial clubs in
England, but he had a drive to be a football manager and to do
the job to the best of his ability.

You need to study and you need to mix with higher level
coaches and learn from them. I took the wrong path and there
was no motivation to grow and progress. I chose to stagnate by
opting for drinking and gambling. Even in my latter stages at
Inverness I became uninterested and chose to allow Duncan
Shearer to take more of the training.

I have often been asked why no one at Caley Thistle ever
asked to discuss my problems.

Rightly or wrongly, I believe my defects were overlooked
because I was successful. Perhaps, too, I was reasonably profi-
cient at concealing my worries, even though they were gnawing
away at me inside. I believed I was seen simply as a bit of a rogue,
a guy who loved a good bucketful. I recognised, too, that, under
the influence of alcohol, I was regarded as a bit of a pain in the
arse.

I never let anyone in. Occasionally, over the years, I would
have a heart to heart with Oshor Williams, the long-standing,
and certainly long-suffering friend I met when he and I were
Manchester United rookies, or my brother-in-law Donald
Macaulay, always ready to hear my hard-luck tales. My brother
Andy – Pep to my Pele – would also allow me to offload my
confessions.

A few of my mates in Manchester have been on the receiving
end of my borrowing and my deceit. There are five friends I
see in that city and they know the depth of my difficulties and
my subsequent depression. Three of them, Jon Law, Mick

Connolly, and my old pal, Nige Smith, gave me £10,000 to pay off creditors. I am indebted to them, of course, and grateful for their help. Except it wasn't help; it was another way of feeding my gambling habit. Those loans have still to be repaid and I feel ashamed that I have not yet the means to settle them.

24

No to Thompson and Tannadice

Towards the end of 2002, with my debts spiralling out of control, the opportunity to move my career on to a higher level was presented to me by Eddie Thompson, the charismatic chairman of Dundee United, who sadly died of cancer in October 2008.

It was my third season in Division One. I was an established and prominent figure in Scottish football management and, alongside Ian McCall – then at Falkirk – I was seen as an up-and-coming coach with a big future.

Paul Cherry, one of my former players and by then an agent, contacted me and suggested Dundee United were about to offload Alex Smith, a highly-respected manager who had had a string of bad results.

'I think they might be interested in you,' Cherry insisted. 'Would you be keen to talk to them?'

Of course I was. Paul acted as a go-between, though he wasn't my agent. It had never occurred to me to hire an agent.

I thought little more of our conversation until I received a call from Thompson. He was 'sounding me out' before, presumably, making an official approach to Caley Thistle. He laid out his hopes, aspirations and ambitions for his beloved Dundee United and prodded me for my thoughts on whether I felt capable of leading the team, at that time rock bottom of the SPL, to success.

This was a big club and would have represented a major step up in my career. Thompson, an enthusiastic and effervescent man, particularly on the subject of the Arabs (as United are known) made the job sound extremely attractive. On one occasion he called me on my mobile as part of this 'feeling out' process. I was surrounded by members of my coaching staff and was concerned they might hear his effervescence coming through. I took no chances and moved out of the office and on to the pitch to take the call.

In those early conversations, he made it clear that the job was mine for the taking. He listened to and liked my ideas on how to take United forward. I even went as far as mentioning players at Inverness whom I thought would do a job at Tannadice. Barry Robson was certainly one and, in time, that's where he landed. Duncan Shearer, I informed Thompson, would join me on Tayside and our telephone chit-chat progressed to discussing my contract which, as it turned out, was a very attractive package – a three-and-a-half year deal at £180,000 a year basic, with incentive bonuses on top. I was flabbergasted at such an offer and, of course, my thoughts turned to being in a position to pay off all my debts and start afresh.

I had no thoughts about trying to negotiate any part of that proposal and, on the telephone, I accepted the verbal offer from a man with a genuine love of Dundee United, a love under-scored by the millions of pounds of his own money that he had ploughed into the club.

We agreed to meet the following Sunday, our first face-to-face meeting together. We were to rubber-stamp the contract, after which he would make the official approach to Inverness. Of course, this was the wrong way round and, at least in football terms, highly illegal.

'I want to take up your offer. I will speak to Caley Thistle and we'll meet on Sunday in Perth,' I told him.

By then, Mandy had left me, and my personal circumstances were far from perfect. My private life was in tatters.

We played on Saturday, by which time there was a great deal of media speculation that United were chasing me and Ian

McCall. Unknown to the sportswriters, I had already agreed to take over from Alex Smith, who had been sacked from Tannadice in the first week of October 2002, while Paul Hegarty, a great servant as a player with United, was temporarily placed in charge of the team.

With the offer on the table and thoughts of my meeting with Thompson the following day on my mind, that Saturday night I went for drink in the Heathmount Hotel in Inverness with Graeme Bennett, the Caley Thistle director of football. It was during our chat that I informed him of the approach from Eddie Thompson and how I had agreed to join Dundee United.

But by then, I was having second thoughts. I would have needed to move to the Dundee area, which would have meant me either taking my daughters with me or leaving them with Mandy. They were living in the marital home in Garmouth while I had moved in with my mother in Mosstodloch, three miles away.

Dundee might have been dubbed the City of Discovery, but I was concerned that I might discover I had made a mistake by relocating there.

Maybe it would be better to sit tight, I thought. I was at the top of the First Division with Caley. I could win promotion and be in the Premier League the following season. Such an achievement would boost my stock ever higher.

Bennett's response was straightforward as he launched an offensive to try and persuade me to stay in Inverness. 'We'll give you a four-year contract at £70,000-a-year and you could organise a testimonial year which could bring you tens of thousands of pounds more.' It was tempting.

I agreed there and then in that bar to stay on at Caley for considerably less than half of what was on the table at Tannadice. I called Thompson almost immediately and announced my decision, my new decision. He was not happy and he made it clear.

'I'm really sorry to piss you about,' I apologised, 'but I've had a re-think. My personal situation means I think it's better for me to remain at Inverness.'

He was stunned that I had gone back on my word and he was disappointed because I had been his first choice, he stressed. He put the phone down. It had been leaked that I had rejected United's offer, and a few days later Thompson went before the media at a news conference and flashed my curriculum vitae, which he wrongly claimed was part of my application. I could understand why he did it but I had never at any time applied for that job. Indeed, I have never applied for any job in football management. Paul Hegarty was quickly named the United manager but lasted only 14 games before being ousted in favour of Ian McCall, himself to be a Thompson casualty in March 2005.

The circumstances involving the approach from Thompson embarrassed him, I'm sure, and I regret that. But when he announced his appointment of Hegarty, it came just 24 hours after he insisted he had never spoken to me. He attacked Caley Thistle and Graeme Bennett, who had revealed the United approach to the media.

Thompson denied that United had ever had any contact with Inverness that he had ever spoken to Bennett, and when he was asked to confirm that he had made no contact with me, or a representative, he said this was correct. He claimed in a strongly worded attack on Inverness that United had been 'used' by the First Division club and he was adamant that 'Hegarty is the first person to be offered the job since I came in here as chairman'.

I remember explaining to the media that Thompson's version of events was inaccurate. I had accepted a job offer from the Tannadice chairman before an official approach was made to Inverness Caledonian Thistle, I announced.

I told the assembled members of the Inverness press that Thompson's outburst had forced me into spilling the beans on his unofficial contact with me and that my integrity was intact. I needed to put the record straight.

This was my official statement on an issue that became rather messy:

> The fact is I had a couple of conversations throughout last week with the Dundee United chairman, and also with an agent, and I accepted the post of Dundee United manager.
>
> I was to sign a contract on Sunday in Perth and be unveiled as manager on the Monday. I met with Graeme Bennett and I had a long heart-to-heart about my circumstances at the club and my own personal situation.
>
> I had a sleepless night on Friday and by Saturday at about 6 p.m. I decided that on certain grounds, predominantly family issues, I couldn't go through with the Dundee United offer.
>
> By this time, an agent had contacted Caley Thistle to ask if Mr Thompson could get official permission to speak to the club and myself. By that time, I had made a call myself to the agent and to Mr Thompson directly to say I had to decline the offer. I apologised for putting them in that situation, and that is where we are at now.
>
> I had hoped to keep this confidential out of respect for certain people at both clubs, but unfortunately it has gone further than that. The club here and I have to defend ourselves, the facts and the truth.

Graeme Bennett said Inverness would not make any complaint about the alleged tapping offence.

He added: 'The club is very disappointed it has had to come to this stage. It is a sad day for our club and for Steve Paterson, but the bottom line is that our supporters were entitled to know the truth.'

I don't regret my decision. But at the same time it was nonsensical that I turned down Dundee United yet, within a few weeks, I accepted a bigger, some might say, more prestigious job and while rumours spread like wildfire that my reason for rejecting Thompson's deal was because that other club had already lined me up, I can state categorically that that was not the case.

I often reflect that moving further south to Dundee might have been better. It may have given me the new start in a different town that I needed, far away from the mayhem and turmoil I had created in Moray. I did not know that fate and coincidence were, even then, conspiring to take me on another adventure.

On the other hand, everything seemed to fit for Aberdeen. Duncan Shearer, a big favourite with the Dons fans from his playing days there, would be my assistant; I had rejected Dundee United; the results under Aberdeen's Danish manager Ebbe Skovdahl were unacceptable to the Aberdeen fans; and the club craved a big lift. Duncan and I were confident we could give it what it needed.

25

More debts and Mandy's departure

The strain on me as 2002 drew to a close was enormous. I had racked-up £30,000 of gambling debts and my life, through excessive drinking, was in freefall. My marriage to Mandy had crumbled through my continuous deceit and lies, and my daughters, Jessica and Emily, were living with her. I was a sad and lonely figure putting on a brave face at work as I tried to hide my disastrous lifestyle, spending more and more time in my usual haunts where I sought solace in Guinness and copious glasses of red wine. The pressure was incredible and my mental health was suffering.

Mandy had left me in March 2002, seven months before the Dundee United offer. In that intervening period I was a wreck of a man, a shadow of what I should have been and unrecognisable from the young athlete who joined the great Manchester United 27 years earlier. I was now 44 and struggling to retain my sanity.

Throughout much of my management career, my mood would often be dictated by the result on a Saturday and, of course, whether my bets had come up. Mandy's life with me was intolerable and she had given me her thoughts on that painful issue.

She used to tell me that part of my problem was that my mum kept bailing me out. She reminded me that my mother had even taken out loans to pay off the debts I had built up. Mandy would beg her not to do it.

'The more you do it,' she would say to my mother, 'the more

he'll gamble. Until he's left without money, he'll keep gambling.'

Mandy stopped giving me money when we moved to Garmouth. There were times when she took my credit cards from me but that never worked because I would go into a foul mood until she handed them over.

I always liked a drink but not, as Mandy would testify, with the kind of nastiness in my behaviour that came in more recent years. If we lost a game, she knew I would not be nice to be around. If we drew, she simply wouldn't know what my emotions would be and if we won, she wouldn't see me until the next day. In short, win, lose or draw, it was never a good situation for her.

On a Sunday, I would leave for the newspapers at about eleven o'clock in the morning, frequently having been out all night drinking, and I wouldn't go home until between midnight and 1 a.m. That was every weekend.

I would apologise profusely for my misdemeanours and by Tuesday she would have softened enough to forgive me. On Wednesday and Thursday matters would improve but by the weekend, it was back to square one. She couldn't take it any more and one day she turned to me and said: 'I've had enough. I am going to see a solicitor to discuss a divorce.'

To her credit, she did a great job in raising our girls and, despite her heartache, she kept them away from the arguments and the trouble.

Before we broke up, Mandy met a new man and my emotions were confused and jumbled. I drank even more heavily to try to ease the pain of the problems I had created.

One night I lost the plot and set out for revenge because I felt this man with whom she had taken up had stolen my wife from me. I was so wrapped up in my own mess. Goodness knows how she ever put up with me and my intolerable behaviour.

In a crazed and drunken state, I tried to kick down the door to our Garmouth home, believing the new man in her life was there. The police were called but Mandy refused to press charges. She told them she and I would sort out our difficulties. I was out of control and as low as I had ever felt.

Mandy remembered talking with the CID officer who attended the scene, as they say in the TV cop shows.

'I really can't understand this,' he told her. 'Steve has a beautiful house, a beautiful wife, two lovely kids and a fabulous job. What more could he want?'

In more recent times, now that we are friends, I told Mandy that I had taken away her 20s and part of the 30s of her life and I felt so bad about that. I hope one day she will be able to forgive me.

There were good times with Mandy but even when we went on holiday I would let her down because of my drinking exploits. On one occasion, Mandy was asleep with the girls in our hotel in Ibiza and the management had to call her in the middle of the night to come and persuade me to leave the swimming pool where I had decided to cool off. I was drunk and fully clothed.

As for the incident where I was taken by police from Mandy's house after breaking the door, there was a 'source' from Caley Thistle quoted in the *Daily Record* newspaper as saying: 'The club know the circumstances and the directors are standing by Pele. As far as I know no one else is involved in the split. Everyone up here knows Pele is a man's man and likes the horses and a drink. But that's as far as it goes. The Highlands is a tight-knit community and news travels fast.'

Graeme Bennett was asked to comment on the debacle and he told the newspaper: 'The club are supporting Pele during his marriage difficulties. He has taken a couple of weeks off. We hope they are able to sort things out. What's happening in his personal life will have no effect on his role as manager. We are 100 per cent behind Steve.'

I appreciated the backing of Bennett and the club but it did nothing to remove the embarrassment I felt.

Mandy did not deserve the misery I brought her and our daughters. She had always supported me and was even featured in the newspapers in the immediate aftermath of our famous victory over Celtic in the Scottish Cup at Celtic Park of 2000.

This is what she had to say in those happier times: 'Steve's so laid back that Tommy Docherty once claimed he was liable to fall asleep at any moment. That's maybe not quite true, but there are times when he does my head in because of his refusal to get wound up or be rushed. The players play for him, not for the club. Steve has their respect because he treats them properly. He hates people who shout and bawl.'

By June 2002 our lives were very different and Mandy had met and fallen for a 28-year-old distillery worker called Paul Anderson – the reason for my screaming, shouting rant that night I tried to break down the door. He and his wife, Ceri, had lived just round the corner from us in Garmouth. My marriage to Mandy was over but I found it difficult to accept that she could be with another man and in my darkest moods I frequently thought of vengeance against him, though he was not to blame for anything. I was the creator and perpetrator of all our woes.

The newspapers loved the story of our break-up and of her liaison with Paul.

'A RIGHT INVERMESS – Mrs Super Caley got a bit too pally while husband Pele was out on the swally' was how the *Daily Record* billed their story of June 2002. They ran it in the week Mandy and I were divorced which was bad enough, but what made matters worse was that the new man in Mandy's life was married and had walked out on Ceri, after less than a year of wedded bliss.

It was a terrible time for all concerned and was exacerbated by the fact that I was a well-known figure in Scottish football and therefore a prime target for tabloid news.

They dug up personal issues for public perusal. A so-called friend of Mandy was quoted as saying:

No one knows what she's had to put up with down the years. Mandy is heartbroken about how things have turned out but she also wants to get on with her life. Her marriage to Steve is over, finished, history. There's no way back for them now. She is rebuilding her life with Paul. For the first time in many years, she's receiving some tender loving care and she's thrilled to bits.

She'd taken about as much from Steve as any woman could stand. His drinking exploits were legendary. She used to say his days started and finished on the bar stool at his local pub, the Garmouth Hotel.

He loved it in there and is hero-worshipped by a bunch of hangers-on who would be better friends if they told him to ease up on his drinking.

Of course, I was hurt and wounded by such stories. I also felt guilt that I had brought so much unhappiness and I was pleased to read that, when a *Record* reporter approached her in the street to seek a comment about her affair with her young lover, she exploded, 'It's none of your business, now just leave us alone.'

Our divorce came through on 25 October 2004. Mandy told me that when she walked into the solicitors the day she started proceedings, she was asked: 'What have you got?' Everybody thought that being married to a football manager brought with it riches. The truth is that she used to iron other people's clothes to earn money for herself. Today, we have a good relationship and the past has been laid to rest. This is important in the interests of Jessica and Emily and I accept full responsibility for the difficulties I brought to my family over the years of gambling and drinking.

We'll always have a relationship because we have children and because we've had a major past together. That can't be written off. She has made it clear that if she hadn't broken free, she would never have had a life. I fully understand that.

I was unhappy with my life and how I was stuck in a perpetual spiral of debt and drinking and yet I couldn't bring it to a halt. I began to have blackouts where I couldn't recall what had gone on the night before. From 2000, when my brother, Neil, died after a massive heart attack at the age of just 49, through the following year when pancreatic cancer claimed my father, to 2002 when Mandy left me, it was clear that depression had taken hold of me.

I felt guilt about my relationship with my father, which didn't amount to much until the 1990s when we eventually struck up a bond and socialised together. He probably had his cancer for some time because when he was eventually diagnosed it was so far advanced that he lasted only a short time before he died.

I would visit him on my own at Dr Gray's Hospital in Elgin and talk to him. He helped me financially when I needed it and, certainly when I entered football management, took a keen interest in my career. His passing was a devastating blow to my mother, who had the additional worry and sadness of Neil's death and my gambling habit.

Her whole life was her family and she was always there to support me and listen to my hard-luck stories as I tried to extract cash from her to either pay off a creditor or, more than likely, race to the bookies to place a bet.

There were many occasions when she would endeavour to talk some sense into me but her advice went unheeded and I never considered her feelings as she watched her oldest child and her husband die in successive years.

Neil and I had never been close because of our seven-year age difference. Once an electrician at the Baxters food-processing plant at Fochabers, he was an alcoholic with a drink problem that was different from mine. While I binged at weekends, Neil drank daily, starting in the mornings when he awoke.

To his credit, he fought his disease and was sober for eight years before he died. By then, his marriage had already broken up although he had met a woman with whom he enjoyed a loving relationship. Neil left a son and a daughter who, like all the family, were shocked by his sudden death, especially as he had had no history of heart problems. Maybe his lifestyle – he was a heavy smoker and did little or no exercise save for messing about in his little boat at Hopeman, where he set creels – caught up with him. I think my father felt guilty that his first-born child had died before him.

After the memorable victory over Celtic my world seemed to spiral downwards and I vividly remember concealing my un-happiness. Bereavements, marriage at breaking point, constant gambling and my drinking; all these components conspired to wear me down. Psychologically, I wasn't in a good place and there were times at training that I felt ill at ease and I began to acknowledge that everything was piling up and leading me further down the road to misery. The last thing I needed was to take charge of one of Scotland's biggest teams.

26

Aberdeen calls at a bad time

In December of 2002, after rebuffing Dundee United and coming to terms with having lost Mandy, I began to feel more settled. I was named First Division Manager of the Month for November, my third in a row. At the same time, the news came through that Aberdeen had sacked Ebbe Skovdahl. Within days the north-east club's search for a new manager would thrust me into the spotlight, just where I didn't want to be with my chaotic private life.

Duncan and I had already agreed to sign long-term deals with Inverness Caledonian Thistle but it did not stop Stewart Milne, the multi-millionaire chairman of Aberdeen, approaching my employers for permission to speak to me. Naturally, I was flattered, and when I told Duncan he was as excited as a young boy about to play his first game for the school team. However, with all that was going on in my life, part of me wanted a period where I could simply settle and get on with my job at a club where I felt comfortable and held in high regard.

I agreed to meet Milne at his luxury home in the leafy suburbs of Aberdeen to hear what he had to say. He made it clear that he wanted the matter tied up as quickly as possible and I could understand that, given Skovdahl's failure with the Dons team and the clamour of the supporters to bring in someone who could restore lost pride.

I took Innes Smith, an accountant friend from Garmouth, with me to the meeting. I saw him as a prospective adviser on financial matters, but if truth be known, his expertise was not brought into play. Still, I felt better that I wasn't on my own.

Innes looked the part. He was smart and articulate and had connections with Aberdeen Asset Management, the global investment management group whose boss, Martin Gilbert, was a director of the football club. I was pleased to have him alongside me to impress that I wasn't a naïve character with little clue how to negotiate a deal.

There were other representatives of the Pittodrie board at the meeting, including Keith Wyness, the chief executive, who later joined Everton in a similar role. The gathering was cordial and straightforward and at no point did I question any of the contractual issues presented to me.

In the meantime, Caley Thistle tried to persuade Duncan to take over from me at the club but they couldn't compete with the package on the table from Milne. In any case, he saw our partnership as one that could bring back the glory days to a club that had never fully recovered from the departure more than 15 years earlier of Sir Alex Ferguson.

I accepted a six-month rolling contract at £160,000 a year, £20,000 less than Eddie Thompson's Dundee United offer, and without a long-term deal.

There was no real discussion over the terms; it was presented as a take-it-or-leave-it option. With bonuses also up for grabs depending on how high we finished in the league and if trophies were won, I was happy to accept. I was the club's sixth manager in seven years, following Skovdahl, Paul Hegarty, Alex Miller, Roy Aitken and Willie Miller. Exalted company indeed.

The board members were content with my plan for the way forward and satisfied with my proposal that Duncan would be my right-hand man. My good and trusted friend, Oshor Williams, would come on to the coaching staff and I wanted to bring Neil Cooper back to the club to oversee the development of the younger players. I felt that Neil, who had been paid off previously from Pittodrie and was then at Forfar, would not only be a capable coach for the under-19s, but that, as a former Aberdeen player, it could be useful for me to tap into his knowledge of the club and how it worked.

A day or two later, armed with the contracts, Keith Wyness arrived at Innes's house in Garmouth. He was anxious that they be signed immediately. Of course, such important documents also needed the signature of a witness. That witness was Innes's mum, Muranne, who was happy to put pen to paper in her little Garmouth home to seal my move to what was arguably the third biggest outfit in the Scottish Premier League.

The whirlwind nature of my departure from Caley Thistle, very much in contention to become an SPL club the following season, left me dizzy. I'd had seven wonderful years at Inverness but I needed to show that I could be successful at a higher level. It was a massive opportunity for me and one on which I could not have turned my back.

I did my former employers, and Graeme Bennett in particular, a favour before I left. I viewed it as an honourable act after all the support I had received from Inverness. The question of compensation came into play during talks and although I had agreed verbally to a new four-year deal with them, no contract had actually been signed.

Indeed, I was out of contract in May 2003 and basically had around five months left on my agreement with Caley Thistle. This amounted to about £20,000, which Graeme asked me to keep quiet about, and he negotiated a £100,000 compensation fee with Aberdeen plus a pre-season friendly worth something in the order of £30,000.

I could have been a bit of a shark on this issue but money never mattered much to me – had I received that £100,000 as a signing-on fee, it would only have ended up with some lucky bookie.

Caley Thistle had been like a family to me over the years and I knew the Aberdeen compensation package could bolster their promotion push as they led the First Division when I left.

There was a great deal of speculation as to who would replace me, but that was none of my concern. In the end, the job went to the former Hearts and Scotland striker, John Robertson. The beneficiary of much of the effort Duncan and I had put in and the signings we had made, he gained promotion the following season.

The notes I wrote while in the Sporting Chance Clinic tell the story of the escalation and gravity of my drinking after becoming a full-time manager and about the blackouts and loss of memory because of my alcohol abuse.

I have slept on pool tables and pavements and generally on a 'good' night out I don't remember my actions from the night before and often have to ask who I need to apologise to. I have been beaten up on a number of occasions and can't remember a thing leading up to it or who kicked me in. The number of times I could not remember my actions over the years would reach into the thousands.

The Clinic also invited us to address the issue of drinking alone:

This habit began around 1995, just after I'd finished my playing career and begun my first job in full-time management. I would drink alone, usually in my house with bottles of Stella Artois and glasses of red wine. I would sometimes go to a pub on my own as the years progressed. After the pub I would drink as long as I could at home or at someone else's house, usually till I passed out or was sick or a combination of both.

This wasn't on my CV, of course. Had Aberdeen had any inkling of just how bad I could be, they would have given me a wide berth.

27

Running the Dons on the cheap

I was unveiled as the new Aberdeen manager to a gaggle of reporters, photographers and television and radio personnel at a press conference at Pittodrie Stadium on 11 December 2002. It was an occasion which underlined for me just how big a club this was. The Dons were sitting eleventh in the twelve-team Premier League, just six points ahead of bottom club Motherwell. But Stewart Milne was optimistic as he welcomed the media.

'We are delighted to have appointed one of Scotland's brightest young managerial talents,' he said. 'Steve is a very determined character and has a great record of success from his early management days in the Highland League through to his time with Caley Thistle.'

Stewart McKimmie, a member of Sir Alex Ferguson's European Super Cup-winning side in 1983, was quoted as believing I was the man to lead the club out of the doldrums.

'People were calling for another foreign coach,' he pronounced, 'but Steve knows the Scottish game inside out. He has been the fans' favourite to succeed Ebbe Skovdahl from the start and getting the crowd on your side is half the battle at Pittodrie.'

My appointment was big news and while George Burley, the former Ipswich Town and Scotland right-back, was reported two days earlier as saying he would be interested in the Aberdeen job and Bruce Rioch, another ex-Scotland player, was also a contender, I was the person sitting before the cameras on one of the most exciting days of my life.

I soon discovered, however, just how low morale was among the players. Four days later, I took my new team to Dunfermline for a Sunday game and lost 3–0.

My line-up that day was: David Preece; Russell Anderson, Eric Deloumeaux (Chris Clark, 83), Phil McGuire, Jamie McAllister, Kevin McNaughton, Fergus Tiernan, Darren Young, Darren Mackie (Leon Mike, 77), Derek Young, Laurent D'Jaffo (Scott Michie, 83).

My first impressions of the team were not favourable. They lacked many of the qualities I had instilled into my sides over the years. The fighting spirit was poor, there was an absence of leadership, little flair in either midfield or on the flanks, and two strikers who would have struggled to score in a brothel.

Communication, especially at the back, was nonexistent and it was unsurprising that they sat at eleventh in the Premier League. I remember a discussion I had with Duncan about individual players after that debut match and we concluded that Eric Deloumeaux and Phil McGuire lacked stature at the back, that Tiernan was decidedly average in the midfield, and that the Young brothers and D'Jaffo looked a spent force. I concluded that I had left a far better side in the First Division at Inverness. I knew I was going to have my work cut out at Pittodrie.

Could they survive the relegation dogfight? That was to be my principal priority, although another issue uppermost in my mind was my brief to cut the wage bill and to remove those players – signed by my predecessor – who were earning too much.

A number of the squad members came into that category, all being paid salaries of up to £4,000-a-week. The Belgian, Roberto Bisconti was one. So, too, were Peter Kjaer, a highly experienced Danish goalkeeper, Eric Deloumeaux, a midfielder or defender from France who had also played at Motherwell, and another man of many clubs, Laurent D'Jaffo. Ben Thornley, a former Manchester United starlet alongside David Beckham and once regarded as a potential big name of the future, had been with the club for a year when I took over and I could see from the flashy car he drove that he was on a salary beyond his capabilities as a footballer. I later learned that he was involved in the property market in a very big way and was a very well-off young man. But he hadn't done particularly well under Skovdahl and was on my hit-list to be binned.

I could tell very quickly that some players, particularly the foreign contingent, did not buy into me. I could almost read their minds.

'Who is this guy from a First Division club who thinks he can manage a Premier League side?'

The downside to all of this was that the wages ceiling was to drop from the £4,000-a-week Skovdahl had at his disposal, to around £1,000 which, in effect, was asking me to do the job with one hand tied behind my back. Still, those were the terms of the agreement and I set about trying to stabilise the football budget, which had run out of control.

The speed of the whole affair was quite breathtaking. The deal to take me to Pittodrie had been concluded within a few days. What was I letting myself in for? I had not properly prepared myself in terms of having ambitions to take over at a big club. Yet there I was, trying to come to terms with the size of this organisation compared to Inverness in a range of respects: the much bigger support, the numbers of people on the staff in the various departments, the tradition of the club and the big stadium.

The media, too, was something to which I had to accustom myself. At Inverness, I saw two or three newspapermen, did interviews with the local radio station, Moray Firth Radio, and an occasional piece with Grampian Television, then the commercial TV channel for the north of Scotland. It was all rather easy-going and remarkably friendly.

At Aberdeen, of course, a club with a proud history and a

leading SPL outfit, the media scrutiny was constant and power-ful. The tabloids, the two local newspapers – the *Press & Journal* and the *Evening Express* – the national broadsheets, Northsound Radio and Grampian TV, all had to be fed virtually on a daily basis. Sometimes it was an irritant and a part of the job I could have done without – but it was one that had to be done. In some ways it was quite daunting and I hadn't fully realised that the challenge I had taken on was so enormous.

The club had huge debts, the playing staff had failed to deliver for Skovdahl and there was no fizz in the dressing room. One of the attractions I held for Stewart Milne and his board of directors was that they had seen what I had achieved on the limited budget available to me at Caley Thistle and they thought I could replicate that with a larger pot of money – though not the sums that had been placed before a long line of my Pittodrie pre-decessors.

However, taking teams through the leagues, as I had done with Inverness, was quite different from trying to restore the Dons to their former glory.

My view of some of the players was that they were taking money without giving the commitment needed to try to rebuild this once-proud club. There was apathy and despondency in equal measure in the dressing room, especially given their lowly position in the league table.

I embarked on a programme of sorting out the wheat from the chaff and I looked to the First Division, where I believed there were players who could do a decent job for me and within my budget. David Johnston, the club's general manager, and I were to liaise closely during my time at Pittodrie and we would discuss budgets, player recruitment, wages and which players should be moved on. John Kelman was our Glasgow-based chief scout and he tended to spend much of his time watching lower league games in England and would report on which players he felt might be useful to us.

Results were needed fast to stave off further decline in the league. At the same time, we had to drive down the wage bill. Such juxtaposition did not sit easily. I knew that slashing wages, which meant easing certain players out of the Pittodrie exit, limited me.

I had earmarked Barry Robson as a player to bring in but we could not match the salary he was offered at Dundee United, which was a great pity as his talent and strength, allied to his incredible will to win, would have made an enormous difference to the Aberdeen side. Allowing the Tannadice club to pip us for his signature was, in my view, narrow thinking and a great mistake.

There was another player to come on to my radar at Pittodrie who might have done a turn for the Dons. He was a teenager, freed by Southampton, with a reputation of being undisciplined and with fitness levels that weren't acceptable. I was keen on him and spoke with Johnston about trying to bring him to the club, partly because he was free and he would not be in a position to demand a big salary. I also felt he might be the kind of striker we needed.

Johnston spoke with the Southampton manager, Gordon Strachan, then reported to me that he had been advised the player would not be a good signing and our interest, or at least mine as I seemed to be the only one keen to pursue the player, ended.

His name was Scott McDonald. He joined Motherwell, where he scored lots of goals before being signed by Celtic for £650,000 by Gordon Strachan, the same boss who ditched him at Southampton. Who was it who said football's a funny old game?

There was some suggestion at one point that we travel to Stavanger in Norway to take part in a game. I believe it might have had something to do with that city and Aberdeen being linked through the oil industry. The very name 'Stavanger', sent shivers down my spine as I relived that awful day when I was summarily kicked-out of the place when I arrived with Karen, my girlfriend, and was found to be in possession of cannabis, drugs that weren't mine but which were in the holdall I had borrowed from a friend in Manchester.

Norwegian football was to have kick-started my career after the debacle of Sheffield United until it all tuned sour and suddenly I was seen as a druggie who shouldn't be allowed to sully that Scandinavian country.

Take the Aberdeen team where? Friendly? Special game? Good for the club? You must be joking. My mind went into overdrive. What if, upon our arrival, some suspicious customs official took a close look at my passport then drew his eyes down a long list of undesirables? What if I was then invited into a room in the airport, the same room where I had been interviewed all those years earlier? Fucking hell! What if the team and all the other members of the travelling party were waved through while their manager was frog-marched towards the next plane heading for Aberdeen? I was in a cold sweat when this sugges-tion materialised. Oh yes, great, I thought. The papers would have a field day with that story. Thankfully, nothing came of it and my fears disappeared.

My goal was to find players who would wear the Aberdeen jersey with pride, though I knew at a maximum of £1,000 a week, there would be a question over their quality. Paul Sheerin came from Ayr United. He'd been on Celtic's books as a schoolboy then went to Southampton, where he worked under three managers, Ian Branfoot, Alan Ball and Graeme Souness, though he never made a first-team appearance.

I signed midfielder Steve Tosh from Livingston in 2003 and he became a hugely popular figure with the fans. He was experienced and full of energy and enthusiasm and played seventy games scoring nine goals for the Dons. He would, I'm sure, have been pleased to stay on at Pittodrie when his contract expired after I left, but Gretna, then in Division Three, offered him more money. That illustrated the difficulty I faced in attracting, and keeping, quality players.

Ironically, just a few years later, Tosh was to haunt the Dons. He scored the opening goal for Queen of the South in the 2007–08 Scottish Cup semi-final when his side won 4–3, a humiliation for Aberdeen.

Leigh Hinds, a striker who had started his career at Wimbledon, was recruited from Clyde. He proved a big disappointment and never lived up to the expectations I had had of him. Indeed, I once had to fine him two weeks' wages after a nightclub brawl with his former team-mate at Clyde, David Hagen. Hinds apologised for his behaviour but he was offloaded the following year and joined Partick Thistle.

There were other recruits as the board urged me to pursue home-grown talent. The previous path of making big-money signings, mainly of foreign players with extortionate wages, hadn't worked. The new policy would be to try to build a team comprising as many Scottish players as possible and to try and bring others through the ranks. Unfortunately, one of the things that really surprised me about the club was that the youngsters already on the books – the next generation of first-team players – were, with the odd exception, sub-standard.

The only two I thought would progress from the youth system at that time were Zander Diamond, whom I rated highly, and Richard Foster. Both became first-team regulars. I gave Diamond his first-team debut and I made Russell Anderson captain. He epitomised what we were striving to find. He was a local lad who had started out at Pittodrie as a member of the primary schools select, signing as a professional when he left school. He was whole-hearted in his approach to his work. He was a quiet, gentle-natured boy and was a good example to others and certainly good captain material.

Had I had a batch of talented young players ready to step

into the shoes of those expensive flops I had to offload, my managerial life would have been much easier. That was not the case. I was forced to put in young players at times because of injuries, but there was no doubt the quality wasn't there.

As I expected, the club wanted me to move to Aberdeen. Duncan and I initially stayed in a flat until we found our own accommodation. I bought a house in Newmachar, to the north of the city, while Duncan moved to the West End. Despite having an abode in the area, I tended to commute to and from Mosstodloch, where I lived with my mother. That was my home territory and my bolthole. It was where I felt most comfortable and I put in the miles between the Granite City and Mosstodloch in the Mercedes club car which had been bequeathed by Skovdahl.

I felt Duncan and I were making little steps of progress and I kept my gambling and drinking mainly to weekends. Everything was ticking over reasonably nicely until one dreadful night in March 2003, which led to me making headlines and hanging on to my job by my fingernails.

28

Has anybody seen the manager?

I had been very low for six days after learning that Jamie, the 21-year-old son of my good friend, Jon Law, had died in tragic circumstances in Manchester. I was devastated for Jon, his wife Jenny and their daughter, Harriet, and felt deeply for them. After all, we had been pals since our schooldays together in Moray. My mood, therefore, wasn't good as I kept thinking of the pain Jon and his family would be suffering.

The funeral was to be on the Saturday, the day we were to face Dundee at Pittodrie, and it was decided that Oshor would head south to represent me.

On the eve of the Dundee game I had to attend a function in the city to mark the club's centenary. It was a big affair with civic leaders and members of the sport and business communities. I was as well-behaved as I could have been, sipping only on a glass of wine, just to keep a lid on what could happen were I to overdo the alcohol.

It was a pleasant enough evening, even if it wasn't the choice I would normally make for a Friday night's entertainment. As it drew to a close, some of the members of the Pittodrie non-playing staff who were there, fuelled by the free wine that had been on offer, decided they would continue their merry-making and invited me to join them.

My agreement was the initial mistake I made that night. After all, I had a game the following day. Why would I want to go out on the town, in full view of the fans, and join a serious drinking session? And anyway, wasn't I the guy who didn't know when to stop, who would drink till he dropped?

Led by a group who knew the nightlife map of Aberdeen, we visited a few places around the centre of town and, predictably, I was the magnet for drunken fans wishing to chat and to offer to buy me drinks as well as dispense their expertise on team affairs. I had no mechanism which introduced the words 'no thank you' into the conversation and I drank and drank and drank.

Then, with the 3 a.m. closing time, came the suggestion that we continue our session at the home of one of the gang. With an alcohol-intake capacity that even I sometimes find difficult to believe, I graduated from the Guinness I had been consuming all night, to my next favourite tipple, red wine.

Much of the remainder of that night is a blur, if not a total blank, although I recall getting into a taxi with someone and being dropped off at the flat I occupied at the time at around 6.30 a.m, just eight and a half hours before kick-off. It wasn't what the 'code of football managers' would describe as the ideal preparation for an important match. I can't even remember undressing, but I do have a thought that there was a feeling of bliss when I hit the bed.

Everything was fine. But not for long. I had inadvertently left my mobile phone in the house at which I had partied and was therefore oblivious that Duncan was trying to reach me. He ended up ringing the bell and banging on the communal door of the block of flats and buzzing the intercom as he tried to wake me. His endeavours had, I later learned, frantically gone on for some time after numerous calls to my mobile phone proved unsuccessful. There was no landline in the flat. He was consumed with worry and frustration and had given it his best shot before surrendering his efforts.

My slumber was such that a Sherman tank could have been driven through my apartment and I would have known nothing about it. In the end, Duncan had no option but to take charge of the team and tell the Pittodrie hierarchy that I was ill with stomach pains. It started a chain of events that should have blown my career to smithereens.

I awoke at about 2.15 p.m. and went into a blind panic as I realised immediately the enormity of the situation. I was shocked and horrified and had an almighty hangover. Not only had I overslept, I was in no condition to attend the game. I didn't know what to do. This, I believed, was the end of my fledgling career as the manager of Aberdeen Football Club. Meanwhile, down at Pittodrie, Duncan had hatched the stomach pains cover-up story to protect me. But the word was out on the street among the many punters who had seen me legless the previous night, and there were stories that CCTV cameras had picked me up coming out of a variety of pubs and clubs.

It was one of the most shameful incidents of my life. I had it coming and had it happened at Inverness they would have thrown a veil over it and there wouldn't have been the same kind of scrutiny. Now, however, I was among the big boys of the Premier League where the media spotlight had bigger bulbs.

The Dundee game affair had been my first Friday night drinking session in Aberdeen and I simply failed to handle it. Sure, that kind of behaviour went on when I was at Inverness, but I was married and Mandy was always there to ensure I wakened in time. In Aberdeen I was on my own.

The team drew 2–2 with Dundee but that counted for nothing and, as rumours of the real reason I had missed the game surfaced on a fans' website, I was summoned to a meeting with Stewart Milne and Keith Wyness.

Before that, Duncan arrived at the flat with Wyness after the game and I was distraught and in pieces. The magnitude of the story could not be understated. An emergency board meeting was called and it was decided to move quickly to counter speculation. A press conference was arranged for Monday. It was time to face the music . . . and the media.

29

The missing manager: the aftermath

The Pittodrie media room was packed with camera crews, reporters, photographers and journalists all ready to rake over this huge story. A Premier League boss had missed his team's game because he was too drunk.

Had I been sacked I could have escaped, probably abroad for a while, until the dust settled. But the club, perhaps because they were worried that they would be seen in a bad light if they jettisoned me, or maybe because they felt they might be heavily criticised for choosing a pup as their manager, told me they were standing by me as long as I agreed to receive treatment for my drink problem. I was startled. I should have been pointed towards the Pittodrie exit. I could hardly believe I was being given another chance. I was exceedingly grateful, if a trifle bemused.

The media conference was, to put it plainly, harrowing. I was terrified walking into the lion's den and my stomach was churning with nerves. I had to own up that I was an alcoholic and explain what had happened the previous Friday night and Saturday morning. I found the announcement, the questions and the post-conference TV and radio interviews, extremely difficult to deal with. It was one of the worst experiences of my life. I felt low and ashamed and apprehensive that I was about to become a figure of ridicule.

The flash of the cameras and the dazzling lights of the television crews were trained in my direction.

'I am just a human being who is flawed,' I sheepishly told the gathering. 'I hope that the players will still respect me. I don't need a drink all the time but, when I do drink, I don't know when to stop.

'I've been humbled by the club's attitude towards me. Keith Wyness and Stewart Milne have shown kindness and under-standing. I expected, and deserved, to get the sack and I'm sorry that all this has taken away what was a good performance from the boys.'

It seemed silly to add that it was the first time I had missed a game because of drink, but my mind wandered back momen-tarily to that day I missed the Caley Thistle team bus to Falkirk because I had overslept due to over-drinking the night before.

'I prefer to own up to my problem,' I continued, 'and take the professional help I need. The only way I can repay the club is by putting even more effort into turning things around. I felt completely hopeless on Saturday afternoon. I did have stomach cramps, but the problem was drink-induced.'

Every second of that news conference seemed like an eternity. My hands were sweating and I swallowed heavily as nerves and fear gripped me.

Wyness emphasised that the club was backing me and made the point that, had I gone to him in a state of denial, sacking would have been a real consideration. I was so upfront and honest, he announced, that they decided to give me the support I needed. The club would provide all the best professional help available to ensure I was able to prove their faith in me was not misplaced.

'Given the correct professional counselling,' he stressed, 'there is no reason why he can't fulfil his duties as manager of Aberdeen Football Club and we would ask that the fans give Steve their full backing as he confronts a personal problem that unfortu-nately has been seen in sport before. We would ask that the privacy of Steve and his family be respected at what is a very difficult time.'

My knees were still knocking as I was ushered out of that room, my mind a blur and my credibility shot to pieces. My mind was whirring just like those digital cameras inside the media room. Where do I go from here? How can I be taken seriously after that? What would my players and other managers think of this sorry mess?

The radio and TV bulletins flashed the news across the country and the following morning's newspapers carried acres of detail about 'drunk Pele' pledging to make amends. I was heartened by the words of my young captain, Russell Anderson.

'The players are 100 per cent behind the gaffer at what is a difficult time for him,' he stated. 'He has shown great courage in facing the media and admitting he has a problem. We are delighted with the club taking a sympathetic view and giving their support to Steve, backing which is fully reflected in the dressing room.' And it was.

Within football, too, others rallied. There was no condemnation. Many managers made contact to offer sympathy and support. Indeed, I was humbled and taken aback by the level of backing I was given. I remember Martin O'Neill, on a day we faced his Celtic team, shaking my hand and expressing concern for me. He knew what I had was an illness and many other managers took that view. I was one of them and they let me know that.

I also had hundreds of letters from people from all walks of life telling me I wasn't alone in suffering from alcoholism and that they or family and friends had had similar problems. Only the odd letter lambasted me for my behaviour while the vast majority of those who wrote did so with warmth and support for my difficulty. Those letters, from all over the country, were quite overwhelming.

It was a shameful incident. Maybe I should have taken the road to resignation – I had humiliated the club and betrayed their trust in me. I wrestle with that issue regularly.

I went with their advice. They called the shots. I was at their mercy and had I resigned it could have been perceived as running away. But how did I manage? And where did I find the courage to walk out on to Pittodrie at the next home game? It was painful and daunting, more so because I never knew what to expect, but my recollection is that the reception was far from hostile.

Something I took away from Aberdeen at the end of my stay there was that I had not deserved the loyalty of the fans. They never turned on me, not even the following season, when results were poor. At no time did I feel they had cast up the missing manager scenario. Indeed, overall, the fans were remarkably generous in their backing throughout my dodgy reign at Pittodrie.

Of course, there were elements of the support who rightly thought my behaviour that day was disgraceful and they let me know it, whether it was through remarks from the stand or even in the street. But such occasions were rare and I was heartened that those fans were in the minority.

In the meantime, despite my regular counselling session at a private hospital, organised by the club, I could not arrest my twin problems. In short, I was in very bad shape personally and psychologically. I was hiding my drinking and my gambling, and emotionally I was in tatters.

I have to admit that I didn't buy into the counselling provided for me and just told my 'shrink' what he wanted to hear. I went through the motions, although I did cut down on my drinking for a while after that disgraceful episode. The Garmouth pub, however, remained my retreat at weekends, when I continued to consume large quantities of Guinness.

30

Struggling to keep on track

The turnover of dead wood among the playing staff at Pittodrie was rapid. In some ways I was caught in the middle, stranded between the restrictions imposed by the board and the expectations of the fans, who were displeased at the quality of player I was recruiting. Of course, while I wasn't gagged, I couldn't reveal that the financial difficulties of the club dictated the type of squad I could have at my disposal.

I didn't have the experience of handling the media and their incisive questioning on the subject and sometimes I felt like a rabbit caught in the headlights when they would probe and prod. Perhaps there were occasions when I was too open.

Naturally, I would have loved to have had better players join me but it should be remembered that not only was there a cap on wages, but I was also instructed that I could not pay a transfer fee for a player unless it was a nominal amount. This was cheapskate productions and I was looking in the bargain basement for purchases.

I wanted Lee Miller and Mark Kerr from Falkirk. I rated Miller as an outstanding prospect but he chose Bristol City for a fee and a salary we couldn't afford, while Kerr eventually went to Dundee United, again for a higher pay-packet. Ironically, Jimmy Calderwood – my successor at Aberdeen – persuaded Kerr to join the club once his contract at United had expired. He'd previously rescued Miller from the Tannadice club where it was clear he hadn't fitted in. I was also interested in trying to get Stephen McManus on loan from Celtic but that proved a non-starter.

One good piece of business I did was to sign Michael Hart from Livingston. He had been allowed to leave the club under Skovdahl but I had seen a great deal of him when I was with Inverness and I felt he was good enough for the Premier League. As it was, he took some time to re-settle at Pittodrie and didn't do too well in those early days under me. However, he went on to be a tremendous player for the club before he moved to the Coca-Cola Championship with Preston North End.

Another good piece of business I completed was to sign Markus Heikkinen, a powerful defensive midfielder from Finland. He proved a huge asset and later left to join Luton Town before moving the Austrian Bundesliga side, SK Rapid Wien where, in 2009, he was valued at £1.1 million.

From December until the end of that season we did reasonably well, finishing eighth in the Premier League table and I felt there was an air of optimism around Pittodrie.

I spent a great deal of time surveying the market to see which out-of-contract players were available. Every other day I would sit down with David Johnston looking through letters from agents all over Europe trying to sell us this player or that.

I brought Scott Booth back to the club in July 2003. Booth, a local boy, had been a successful striker for the Dons for nine years before joining the German giants, Borussia Dortmund and then moving on to play in Holland for four years, notably with FC Twente.

But Booth's stay was short-lived and I released him the following year, a move which did not endear me to many of the supporters. In an ideal world I would have offered Booth another contract but I couldn't because of the financial constraints imposed on me.

Despite the upset it caused the player and some of the fans, it was interesting that one football writer wrote:

To anyone who had paid attention to Booth's career, no explanation or apology should have been necessary. He is, in truth, an example of a common phenomenon in the game, the player who simply has not made the expected progress or fulfilled the potential of his impressive early days.

In Booth's case, the general failure to deliver has been compounded by lengthy unavailability because of injury throughout his career. It is his manager's misfortune that so few who fall within his province seem to have noticed.

There was one scouting mission to Liverpool where I went to see a young Everton player in action and he impressed me so much that I considered trying to persuade him he could have a future at Aberdeen. His name? Leon Osman. He was a product of Everton's youth system and when I went to watch him in a reserve game he was just getting back into the swing of things after being out for almost a year with a knee injury.

Osman had been at Carlisle on loan and it wasn't looking like he would make an impact at Everton so he was farmed out once more, this time to Derby County. It was just before he went there that he came on to my radar and I liked his midfield play. Nothing came of our interest in Osman, who became a regular in the Everton side and a consistently good performer.

It was at the end of that weekend trip south of the border that I became the centre of another brush with authority, when I was suspected of being a drug dealer.

My sojourn, which must have come at a time when there were no Premier League games because of international matches, was combined with a series of drink-fuelled sessions with my Manchester-based buddies, including Mick Shaw, Jon Law, Nigel Smith and Mick Connolly. Needless to say, our time in the pubs led to visits to a casino where I did particularly well. So well, in fact, that I headed home with £10,000 of winnings stuffed inside my pockets.

I felt on top of the world but didn't reckon on the furore my stash would cause at Manchester Airport where, during the usual security search, the attendant felt various lumps and bumps in my clothing – bundles of bank notes. I was invited into a little office to explain myself.

'That's a lot of money to be carrying around in cash, sir,' said a uniformed man with more than a hint of suspicion in his voice. 'Why do you have so much money on you?'

He did not have to say so, but it was clear from his tone and the looks I received from two other men in the room, that they had made up their minds I was up to no good. Maybe they thought I had sold drugs in Manchester. Or perhaps I was headed for Aberdeen to buy drugs.

'I won the money at the casino,' I told them. They looked at each other, none giving away anything in their eyes or their expressions. I was peppered with questions: Which casino? Where had I been staying? What was my business in Manchester?

'Look, I'm the manager of Aberdeen Football Club and I've been staying with friends.' They took the details of who my friends were and one man left the room, clearly to make a telephone call or two to check my story. Some time later, he returned, this time with a smile on his face. 'Sorry to trouble you, sir. You understand we can't be too careful. Have a pleasant flight . . . and good luck in your next game.'

I hurried on to the plane and had a couple of drinks on what was a short journey, bursting to do with my winnings what I always believed was my destiny, to double or even treble them. Within a couple of weeks the £10,000 was donated to a series of betting shops.

One of my better experiences as manager of Aberdeen came one night in April 2004 when I took a rag-tag of a team to play Celtic at Parkhead, Henrik Larsson et al. The Swedish striker opened the scoring against our inexperienced side and I thought it would open the floodgates for a heavy defeat for us, especially as we had so many youngsters in our line-up.

The previous season, under Skovdahl, Celtic had hit the Dons for seven and I feared a repetition of that result. We eventually hit back through Bryan Prunty before David Zdrilic, our Aussie striker, fired home the winner.

Later, in the players' lounge I received a friendly mouthful from Martin O'Neill, the Celtic manager, who jokingly rebuked me for having the temerity to end his side's staggering run of 77 games undefeated at home, which had included games against some of the giants of European football.

My betting while I was at Aberdeen was more discreet than it had been prior to my going there. On Saturday mornings, for example, I would tend to leave my home in Newmachar and, en route for Pittodrie, I would look in on my brother, Andy, who lived nearby and I would hand him £500 and my fixed-odds coupon and ask him to do the honours for me.

I made a promise to myself that I wouldn't visit bookmakers in Aberdeen, although I did, but only on very rare occasions. I would usually use bookies in Elgin, and Keith Wyness would sometimes hear rumours of drinking exploits in which I was supposed to be the central character. Such stories always proved to be without foundation.

One Saturday night in a pub in Edinburgh, I was joined by some of my friends who had come up from Manchester. I seem to remember our game in the capital was called off at lunchtime.

My friends quickly got into the social swing of things. I had lain low for a number of months mainly by not drinking in Aberdeen. We were in a sports bar somewhere around Edinburgh Castle and had a great time, reminiscing and laughing and generally having a real lads' day and night. The following week word reached the club that a Sunday red-top tabloid was to run a story that I had been running down some of the people with whom I worked at Pittodrie.

I had been recognised by some punters in that Edinburgh pub and engaged in some banter with them. So, when they would state that such-and-such a player was rubbish, I would simply agree and laugh with them. I was drunk, of course, and played along with their game. This was no serious discussion about football. Rather, it was my way of trying to get them off my case. The mobile phone cameras were flashing all round the joint and, as we expected, the story appeared eight days later and claimed I had been slagging-off various people, including Wyness.

It was quite a distance from accuracy, although in the eyes of some, there was no smoke without fire. In the end, the club was satisfied that it had been blown out of proportion.

Wyness came across as an ambitious man who was good at his job. Mind you, it could be argued he didn't do terribly well by recruiting me. He was a modern chief executive and was in tune with the corporate and marketing side of the club which he ran like a business. He did well for Aberdeen.

We had a working relationship that was OK but in reality, I should never have agreed my contract because I had been too naïve, too wet behind the ears at that level, to raise the question of playing budgets and what restrictions there were. Throw in my personal problems and it was a massive error for me to have even considered taking the job.

I was not betting daily at that time but Saturdays were big days for me in terms of my punting while Saturday nights, back among my own people in Garmouth and Fochabers, Elgin, or wherever I chose to release the tension, were all about drinking myself senseless, as my notes from the clinic highlight:

I have felt off track for about 15 years and my friends and family have pointed out how I have changed over the years from a 'happy drunk' to an obnoxious, rude, arrogant bastard when I have a drink in.

Those people I drank with found my inability to recall the nights of a previous evening hilarious. My friends and family, on the other hand, regarded such shenanigans as offensive and never wanted to be in my company when I was drunk. On 15 October 2008, I wrote:

I have lost my motivation and verve for life and my moral values have been blown away by my addiction. I have felt powerless and unable to manage the behaviour, despite recognising the damage and hurt it causes.

31

You're job's safe . . . you're fired

The performances of the Aberdeen team and their poor results piled more and more pressure on me. The reasonably respectable – given the financial constraints – eighth finish the previous season meant nothing. This was a club where the fans had high expectations and they were fed up of having a succession of mediocre sides and managers who could not motivate the players enough for them to win trophies.

It had been a difficult season. We were safe in the second last game of that term when we finished eleventh, last but one. I was already making plans for the following season regarding training preparation, signing targets and players I would release. I'd had meetings with David Johnston about those plans and we had identified players we could bring in.

But one newspaper ran a story speculating that I would be sacked and that Willie Miller, the number one Aberdeen player of all time, according to most of the fans, would be joining the club as director of football. Willie had managed the club for a time soon after he finished playing but was sacked in 1995 and vowed never to be involved with the Dons if Ian Donald, the chairman who had given him his jotters, was still running the show. Fortuitously for Miller, Donald, whose father Dick was a long-time chairman of the club, stepped down three weeks before I was fired, which meant there would be no barriers to a return for the former club captain and legend.

No one around the Pittodrie scene needed reminding of how high Miller's standing was at Aberdeen FC. He had spent his entire playing career there and he and Alex McLeish had formed one of the most potent defensive partnerships in British football. He had been the one to lift the plethora of trophies won under the direction of Sir Alex Ferguson, including the European Cup-Winners' Cup in 1983, when the Dons beat Real Madrid in the final at the Ullevi Stadium in Gothenburg.

Naturally, I was made uneasy by the talk of Miller's return to the club, assuming that I would be discarded along with Duncan and Oshor. A telephone call from my chairman, however, provided solace and encouragement.

'Ignore what you've read in the paper,' he pronounced. 'It's a load of rubbish. You're the manager for next season. Carry on with your plans.'

Such an assurance was good enough for me and I thanked Stewart Milne. I felt it was more than a vote of confidence, especially as all the pre-season schedules for the players and the fitness programme they should follow over the summer, were in place. I was up for the challenge and I was functioning reasonably well. The club had stood by me in my hour of need, for which I was grateful, and I vowed I wouldn't walk away in a cowardly manner after all that. If I were to be sacked, on the other hand, then my future was in the hands of others. I wanted to try my very best to turn things round.

The following Monday, Duncan, Oshor and I were getting ready for training when Keith Wyness phoned down to my office asking me to go upstairs and see him. Duncan and Oshor and I looked at each other with one of them saying: 'That seems a bit ominous.' A Monday morning call from the chief executive hadn't happened before but on the back of the media speculation it made me nervous.

I went upstairs and when I opened the door of Wyness's office there, beside him, was the chairman.

'Steve, I hate doing this,' Milne said, 'but I have bad news for you.'

He didn't have to say much more. I was shocked, but not enough to prevent me from expressing my feelings. 'It was only a few days ago you told me I was safe,' I raged at him. 'You could have done this differently. You could have told me last week when the story was in the paper. You lied to me.'

From his point of view, of course, there was no easy way to sack me. He had to plan for the good of the club. At that point, though, I felt that I had been led along. I was dejected but I had no argument with the decision. I might have been restricted financially in how I could do my job but there was no doubt that ending the season in such a lowly position and failing to produce the minor miracles expected of me without a great deal of money for players, brought about Milne's decision. I kept the club up and that was the only consolation. It was the shock of the event that day in Wyness's room more than anything else that made me angry.

Looking back, however, I understand their predicament. It was down to me and the outcome was my responsibility. Had I managed that club properly and honestly and done my job in the right way, I might still have been fired but it would have been for the kind of reasons managers are generally sacked, a lack of results. Given the circumstances, I could accept the disquiet that might have been caused had Aberdeen been left in my hands for another season or two.

I arrived back in my office minutes after my multi-millionaire boss had said: 'You're fired!' Duncan and Oshor could tell instantly something was badly wrong.

'The bullet,' I mumbled. Duncan, then Oshor, were summoned individually to see Wyness and were told their fate. They, too, were out. I had let them down badly. They had worked hard and did their jobs properly, giving 100 per cent. I hadn't. It was unfair to them and I feel guilty to this day over what happened. It was the first time I had ever been sacked in almost 20 years in football. It wasn't a bad run.

Milne and Wyness had to look at the overall picture and acted in the best interests of Aberdeen Football Club. As for me, my state of mind was far from good. I was in a bad place.

My anger was aimed at the chairman and the chief executive, a natural reaction. However, I quickly resigned myself to accepting that they did what they had to do and it was clear there were systems already in place to move the club on.

Miller was unveiled at a press conference soon after the Paterson regime was declared finished, and while Duncan and Oshor walked out of the front door to face a barrage of photographers as the news filtered out that we were now ex-employees, I chose a different way of departing the Dons . . . in the boot of a car.

Within an hour or so of receiving my marching orders I decided I could not face the waiting paparazzi as I didn't want my mother and my daughters seeing pictures of me traipsing out of Pittodrie carrying bin bags containing my belongings. My thoughts were simply to protect them, although in my negativity I introduced other thoughts.

'I'm fucked if I'm having those bastards making money out of my misery,' I said of the press photographers to no one in particular.

I spoke with John Morgan, the club's security chief, and suggested a car should be brought into the stadium in order that I could be driven straight out. When the car, a Mercedes, arrived, I loaded my bin bags into the boot and a thought flashed through my mind that, were I also in the boot and out of sight, the photographers wouldn't even know I was in the vehicle.

With Morgan's deputy, Peter Simpson, now sadly dead, at the wheel, I left Pittodrie for the last time in the most unceremonious of methods. Has there ever been such a bizarre departure of a football manager from a club which has just sacked him?

The drive wasn't too far, to the beach area, around a quarter of a mile from Pittodrie. God only knows what anyone witnessing a 6ft 2in tall man emerging from the boot of a car on Aberdeen's beach esplanade would have made of such a scene. My own car had also been driven round to rendezvous with us and I transferred my worldly goods into the back of that vehicle.

I believed the whole sacking affair had been handled badly by the club. They could have had a press conference with me present to announce the parting of the ways with them giving their reasons, while I would have been permitted my say, which would have included an acceptance of the situation. But it was all cloak and dagger stuff and carried through with great haste.

What I thought was going to be a normal day at the football club turned into a major shock, given the reassurance from the chairman the previous week. Of course, it was the dreaded 'vote of confidence' many managers have come to know.

Interestingly, Simon Buckland, a football writer on the *Sunday Times Scotland*, interviewed Miller on 30 May, less than a week later, where there was a reticence by him to reveal how much he might have had to do with my sacking.

Buckland wrote that the chairman had been willing to give me another year, despite the team having lost our last five games of the season, to see if I could make a difference. Miller was less willing.

He told Buckland:

The board felt, 'Are we going to get the best out of Willie with our choice of manager or are we better to give him the freedom to bring in his own choice and style of manager?'

If the board decision was to work with the last manager then that's fine, but I can understand their reasons for not wanting to go down that road because it does give the club a fresh start for my recommendation.

Once Miller had agreed to come on board, Jimmy Calderwood, who must have been in his mind as my replacement, was soon in situ – just four days after Duncan, Oshor and I were booted out. I was the sixth Aberdeen managerial casualty in less than ten years, since Ian Donald had decided that Miller wasn't good enough in the job. Now Miller was instrumental in me losing mine.

I hadn't seen my sacking coming because of Milne's verbal assurance that my job was safe and because he urged me to ignore press speculation that I was headed for the dole.

Maybe my means of escape that day summed up where I was in terms of how I felt about myself and my failure.

Soon after, I had a call from a member of the administration staff at Pittodrie informing me a cheque for six months' salary – £77,000 – was on its way.

I was hugely in debt, the arrears growing by the day because I was out of control with gambling. I had recently bought a house in Fochabers on the back of being the Aberdeen manager and I already had a place in Newmachar, near the Granite City. I was now out of a job and, on top of everything else, without an income.

I was still so hacked-off with being booted out that I gave little or no thought to the possibility that the compensation money could help me pay off my debts. Dejection took over and my drinking became heavier and more frequent, accelerating rapidly as the days and weeks went by. I convinced myself that I had been shafted by Stewart Milne. Yet, anyone with any sense who looked at the big picture would have recognised that he was right to do what he did.

Meanwhile, I accepted all the sympathy that was going, along with the drinks that were offered by whoever happened to be in whatever pub I buried myself in on any day of the week. My depression worsened. I knew my life hadn't been right for a number of years and that I had been lying to myself and behaving irrationally and in a shameful way with my family. I was, indeed, the architect of my own destruction.

Duncan and Oshor, as loyal comrades as you could wish for, were both concerned about my gambling, but probably took the view that it was my choice and my money and that as long as I was discreet, there might not be too much of a problem. But by committing themselves and their families to me by moving lock, stock and barrel to Aberdeen, I had badly let them down.

My eldest daughter, Jessica, was living with my mother and I had a responsibility to her, which is why I lived most of my time, even when I was employed by Aberdeen, in Mosstodloch. My house in Newmachar lay empty. While Jessica chose to remain with me, Emily was too young to be separated from her mother and she went with Mandy and Paul – by then her husband – to his hometown of Falkirk.

I think the embarrassing and highly public incident when I was arrested, prompted them to move away from the area at a time when the atmosphere was rather toxic. Mandy and Paul now have a daughter and I'm pleased to say that we are all friends. They moved back to Elgin in 2007 and have settled in Moray. Emily moved back in with me and Jessica in Fochabers.

Looking back on my 18-month period at Aberdeen, there were many positives to be found in that troubled reign. I had cut the wage bill by around £1m and cleared out the high-earning, non-committed players.

The new manager had been left a good platform from which to build for the following season. It proved that with a bit more investment and permission to pay higher wages to recruit players of the standard of Scott Severin and Barry Nicholson, that a decent team could have been assembled. Unfortunately, I never had access to funds for either transfer fees or wages for such quality players, both of whom were signed by Jimmy Calderwood.

32

Dangerous nights and Lee Westwood's success

Occasionally, in my darkest moments, thoughts of ending my life have danced around my mind. Cowardice and selfishness would never allow such a drastic measure. I used to think of climbing a mountain and drinking booze and swallowing pills and lying down to allow the elements to take me. Thinking was as far as it got.

I have, however, engaged in some stupid and dangerous behaviour which might have resulted in my slipping off this mortal coil, including one hairy incident just before I entered the clinic.

I had been drinking for a couple of days and met a young guy I knew in a pub one night. His name was 'Pav' Munro.

We decided to go on an expedition up the River Spey. It was around 3 a.m. on a bitterly cold September night when we packed half a dozen bottles of wine and trekked about half a mile up river. I was suffering from cracked ribs at the time following a drunken fall so I was in a good deal of pain, although the vast quantities of alcohol I had shipped over the previous 48 hours had helped take my mind off the damage I'd done.

We sat by the river with only the moon for light, and drank our wine and talked and laughed. Then, for some inexplicable reason, I decided I would swim in the raging waters to the other side. And this at a spot where over many years several people had lost their lives. The Spey was in spate, though this did nothing to dampen my enthusiasm for the daring task. I stripped off down to my boxer shorts and jumped into the fast-flowing and treacherous river. The freezing waters rushed over my shaking body and I threw myself forward to begin my swim.

God must have been with me that night as somehow I managed to reach the other side.

'Come on,' I shouted across to the bank from whence I came. 'You can do it.'

My companion walked down river to a less dangerous entry point and, treading carefully in the dark, he slowly waded over. We were both out of our minds with drink and we could easily have died. Had he lost his life, it would have been my responsibility. I instigated this crazy prank. I led this madness.

We walked into the village at around 7 a.m. after trudging for hours back up the other side of the river and wearing only boxer shorts. A local man, walking his dog, passed us by and stared in disbelief.

By then, I was drunk every day. There was no conscious effort to commit suicide but my behaviour was certainly dangerous enough to have ended with me losing my life or perhaps causing someone else to die through my incredible actions.

I was erratic and uncaring about the company I kept. Through a haze, I recall being with a group of drug addicts who were shooting up as I drank. I had ended up in a house a few miles away from Fochabers, a player in this grubby and seedy scene.

Where do I go now? As well as others becoming weary of me and my behaviour I had become tired of myself and of what I had been doing.

If I had been able to sort myself out and had arrested my twin addictions I could have gone back into football management and been there today. But instead of accepting my sacking as a wake-up call, I let it lead to a drastic deterioration in my behaviour and my state of mind.

I started drinking and gambling daily, a rapid road to ruin. The

£77,000 I received from the club was gone in a matter of months. How could it have lasted when I was betting as if I had a bottomless pit of money?

My biggest stake was £10,000 on France to win Euro 2004 in Portugal. They were the title-holders and favourites to retain the trophy until coming up against Greece in the quarter-finals. Who would have predicted a Greek victory, let alone that the rank outsiders would go on to win the tournament? Along with France's pathetic performance went my ten grand. Still, there was plenty more where that came from as once more I lined the pockets of those running the betting industry.

Of course, everything is relative and there are English Premier League players earning tens of thousands of pounds a week who would regard such a bet as chicken-feed. If you have £1m you might place £50,000 on one bet. The money I earned from football and, before going full-time, my wages from the combination of football and social work, allowed me to place higher bets than the average punter.

I had credit cards, too, and I managed to bob and weave, trying to keep all the balls in the air, if only temporarily.

Hard on the heels of the Euro 2004 loss I hit the jackpot with bets on the Open Golf Championship at Royal Troon and raised my eyes towards heaven to thank the good Lord.

Lee Westwood, the young English golfer, was the focus of one my main bets. I placed £2,000 on him at 14/1 to be the top European player in the tournament. He delivered, finishing fourth overall and giving me £28,000 plus my stake. I also had bets on the individual three-man matches in the tournament and by the final day I had amassed £50,000. Such a sum could have taken away the pain of having to lose my house in Fochabers because of mortgage arrears, and might even have recovered the grim situation of substantial debt.

But a major part of my hopelessness with gambling was that, while I would recognise golden opportunities to reduce my debts with big wins, I could never bring myself to hand over the cash to the people and institutions I owed. It was never going to happen.

I've had as much as £20,000 in cash in my house but, rather than pay outstanding bills, I have seen that as my gambling money. When I had those £50,000 winnings from the Open, for example, it just meant that my stakes on other golf tournaments increased to £5,000 a time. All I thought about doing with that money was to gamble it.

In 1974 it was the £1,000 back-hander from Manchester United for agreeing to join them. In 1986 it was the £30,000 pay-off from Japan. In 2004, the £77,000 severance from Aberdeen Football Club. Such a familiar pattern.

Because I was always a heavy gambler, one without fear of losing, I was at my most vulnerable when I had a couple of thousand pounds or more available. I would never dream of betting a fiver on a horse. That wouldn't give me the excitement I needed. If I had £100, on the other hand, I would see that simply as an opportunity to win a sizeable amount to allow me to place higher stakes on other bets. Needless to say, it was only a matter of a few weeks before my fortune from Royal Troon had evaporated.

33

Heading for rock bottom

The house in Fochabers had to be sold as my debts mounted. My ducking-and-diving ran out of steam and the credit cards hit the £100,000 mark. In my clearer moments I think I could have steadied the ship, paid off debts and stayed in the game, perhaps in the lower leagues in England. But it turned into such a black period. Instead of ringing alarm bells and forcing me to bite the bullet and change my ways, it fuelled my worst habits.

My record as a manager before going to Aberdeen was almost impeccable and I believed another club might have seen that and perhaps have been prepared to take a chance on me. The warnings I had, including the sacking from Aberdeen, weren't heeded. Rather, they hurled me faster down the slope of despair, depression and drinking – peppered, of course, with everyday trips to the bookmaker, any bookmaker. I saw no way out of my serious debt problem. Yet still I refused to face up to the chaos I had created.

I obtained the phone number of the Sporting Chance Clinic and my family and Oshor and Jon Law urged me to take the action they knew was required if I were to survive. They were concerned about my state of mind but, in truth, you have to help yourself. I didn't. I overreacted to the sacking. It had been a miserable 18 months for me at Aberdeen, a complete disaster.

Here was a washed-up person who was a former professional footballer and an ex-Premier League manager who spent too much time in the bar of the Garmouth Hotel, that quaint, white-washed old building in a pretty Moray village. The stories of the idiotic things I've done in and around that bar are legend. It was like a second home to me.

I recall one day when, so drunk I could hardly walk, I decided to take a bike – I haven't a clue who it belonged to – from outside the pub and set off to see my girlfriend, Terri Leith, who lived locally. Peddling like fury, the inevitable happened. I lost control and fell off and my little finger was mashed in either the chain or one of the wheels. I was so befuddled I couldn't really tell, but the pain certainly sent me a message that the injury was bad. In fact, when I looked at it I could see my pinkie was hanging off. Someone called an ambulance for me to be taken to Accident and Emergency in Elgin. The demon drink had struck again.

Terri had entered my life in 2002, several months after Mandy and I had split up. It was a bleak time with the marriage break-up and my dreadful behaviour. My private life was at rock-bottom when I met Terri in the Garmouth Hotel in the summer of that year. She was a single girl, 17 years my junior. She was someone who gave me comfort and looked after me and we quickly grew very fond of each other.

Over the months that followed she was by my side and supported me. She wasn't interested in the fact that I was a football manager. She took me for who I was but, just as I did with Mandy, I let her down too many times. It's the story of my life, really. Terri put up with my drunken behaviour for so long before accepting there was nothing she could do to make me change my ways. We each had our own homes, mine in Fochabers, hers in Garmouth, and we stayed with each other in both houses at different times without actually moving in together. We separated in 2007 for a few months but resumed our relationship before it finished for good in 2008. Even today, I find discussing Terri very painful. I deeply regret the distress I caused her.

She meant so much to me and she was unfortunate that she took up with a man who, at that time, was nowhere near the kind of person he should have been. Terri came into my life at the height of my problems and was decidedly short-changed in a relationship where I concerned myself too much with the pursuits that led to my personal and professional demise.

34

Another chance at management

Not long after I left Aberdeen I took a job as a social worker on a temporary basis and in January 2005 I was offered the chance to manage Forres Mechanics in the Highland League.

George Minty was the chairman and he contacted me to sound me out. Unaware of the extent of my personal problems, he may have thought I was looking to re-enter football at a higher level than the Highland League, but told me he'd taken a chance on approaching me to see if going back to Forres might appeal.

My reputation had been tarnished forever in terms of my getting back into the game at a higher level, although George thought otherwise, and anyway, I had a soft spot for the town of Forres. My father had gone to school there and I had won the championship as a player with Mechanics. There was an affinity there and so I joined them at the turn of 2005 and I spent a happy season and a half with them.

Although I was on anti-depressant medication when I was with the club, I really enjoyed my spell there. Part-time football is more social and it was good to get back to my roots; a bit of the craic in training and, of course, the post-match drinking sessions with the players.

My full season took us to fourth in the league, thanks, in part, to a benefactor who put money into the club which allowed me to get better players in by offering good signing-on fees.

At the end of my first season, when I had been in charge for only four months or so, we went as a group to Dublin. It was the club's way of thanking the playing and coaching staff for their efforts throughout the season and was seen as a gigantic piss-up.

Before teaming up with the rest of the travelling party in Fochabers, I had been drinking most of the previous night and joined in with the rest of the lads as we got stuck in to a very large carry-out on the team bus all the way down to Aberdeen airport. There was more booze on the flight, followed by bucketfuls of Guinness that night in the Irish capital. On top of that, I was still taking medication, so you can imagine what kind of state I was in.

At one point I joined a street busker and started singing the Bob Marley songs I knew and danced around to the reggae rhythm collecting money in the singer's Rasta hat.

The next day, goodness knows at what time, I awoke in my hotel room, groggy and with an industrial hangover. I staggered towards the window. When I looked out, I panicked. Was I dead, or in the middle of a bad dream? There in the busy street below, were people dressed in clothes which looked from a bygone era. There were horses and carts and vehicles which didn't belong in the twenty-first century. Was I going insane?

I was confused and found it hard to come to terms with what I was witnessing. Maybe I had flipped, I thought. The drink has, after all these years, caught up with me. I dressed and hurried down to the hotel lobby, my head spinning from the large quantities of alcohol that had passed down my throat.

I can't tell you my relief when I was told the street outside the hotel had been transformed into the set for the re-make of the movie, *Lassie*. And here was me thinking I had gone to sleep only to awake in another time.

For the forthcoming season I decided to back my own ability with Forres. At the end of the 2004–05 season the team had finished around mid-table. I believed we could do better and in the bookmakers' handicap for 2005–06, Forres had a handicap of +19 points.

My Manchester pals and I spread the bets and put stacks of money on the Can-Cans. We stood to win around £80,000, with me taking half of that because of the sums I had bet. For much of that season we were on course to collect, but we lost it in the final week of the season. We came second in the handicap and had to settle for a 'what might have been' tale.

I was on decent money for the Highland League. I guided the team into fourth place but when a new chairman arrived, Dr James Anderson, he painted a new financial picture; the club had been living outwith their means by paying me too much and buying players they couldn't afford.

A few weeks before the end of the season he informed me the club couldn't sustain the outgoings. I was asked to take a wage cut and that we couldn't afford the kind of signing-on fees of the previous season for the players I wanted to bring in. I decided I couldn't do the job justice. I wanted to be challenging for the league championship and I knew I couldn't do it with such restrictions. I quit. Some months passed when Peterhead, then in Division Two, came calling in October 2006.

My flirtation with the Blue Toon club lasted barely 16 months as I accepted my inability to focus on the job in hand. Yet another failed opportunity to make a mark in football management sent me once more into oblivion. It also irrevocably damaged my relationship with a player who had worked wonders for me at Inverness Caledonian Thistle.

Rodger Morrison, the Peterhead chairman and a successful businessman in the Aberdeenshire town, was ambitious for his club. He had guided them from the Highland League into the Scottish Football League and, under Iain Stewart, they had won promotion to the Second Division.

Iain's prowess as a goalscorer, highlighted earlier in this book, was second to none and he was undoubtedly one of the best players I ever had the privilege to manage. But, for some strange reason, despite him steering the club to a mid-table position, taking them to the play-off stages the previous season, and establishing Peterhead as a Division Two side, it wasn't good enough for Morrison. He wanted the club in Division One and took the view that Iain didn't have what was needed to achieve that.

The chairman contacted me, asked me if I was interested in the job and set up a meeting on the morning of a Peterhead match. He told me that what I had done at Inverness, winning promotion through the leagues on tight budgets, was what he wanted for his club, now in a new stadium, Balmoor. I could do that, I told him, as he informed me that Iain would be leaving.

In retrospect, I made a mistake in agreeing to that meeting at a point when Iain was still in place as manager, but it's the way of football and I was an out-of-work manager. Anyway, Rodger had made up his mind over the issue. Iain was sacked, an incredibly harsh decision given his outstanding record with the club, and I was named as his replacement. It was a move that brought about the end of our friendship.

He telephoned me and expressed anger and felt, to quote his words, that I had shafted him. His tirade was understandable but his grievance should have been with Morrison and the Peterhead board. I had made no moves for the job but simply responded positively to their approach.

Iain was bitter and suggested that I had done the dirty on him and, looking back, he may have had a case. Perhaps I was morally wrong. It would have been better, from my point of view at least, had he been sacked first before my services were sought. In any case I am not proud of that particular episode and it certainly wasn't a pleasant situation in which I found myself.

I was appointed on 29 October 2006 and, because Duncan Shearer was, by then, living in Inverness and managing Buckie Thistle in the Highland League, I had to look elsewhere for a full-time assistant. My thoughts turned to Neale Cooper, once a rival manager when I was at Caley Thistle and he was in charge at Ross County.

Neale, a hugely important player when Aberdeen carried all before them under Sir Alex Ferguson, and who later plied his trade at Aston Villa and at Rangers, was out of football management after leaving Gillingham almost a year earlier. Neale had previously managed Hartlepool United when they were in League Two in England, and just failed to win them promotion in the play-offs.

'Neale Cooper would be good to have on board,' I suggested to the chairman. 'He's experienced, has done well with the clubs he has managed and will be good on the training pitch.' I was right. Neale came in and gave it his all, which is more than could be said of me.

Morrison's aim was to move Peterhead into the First Division and while Neale and I were to be full-time, the players would be part-time, an arrangement which really didn't work.

I also brought Dave McGinlay – brother of the Scottish international striker John – on board as coach. Dave had played for me at a number of clubs including Caley Thistle and knew the ropes.

The problem with Peterhead, however, was that it didn't have a sufficiently big fan base, and the infrastructure of the club did not lend itself to participating at a higher level. Although drinking wasn't a big problem for me then, gambling was, and I just couldn't get out of the bit, losing heavily and borrowing to either pay off major debts or simply place some more bets.

I was being paid around £700 a week and Neale, too, was on a good salary, but the difficulties lay in the fact that we had to carry out our coaching in the evening, which meant daytime hours of doing very little other than occasional visits to schools and addressing the youth development programme at the club.

I admit to becoming disillusioned, not just with Peterhead Football Club but with myself. My heart wasn't in the job and the money they paid me – I confess to not giving them a fair return for an excellent salary – was going where it always went, to whichever bookie took my fancy.

Rodger Morrison and his fellow directors treated me well. I let them and myself down and I regret that. Our results weren't too bad but I couldn't see the players I had as being capable of taking the club out of the Second Division. I did bring in new faces, and I believed they were better than the ones already there but, in truth, they proved a disappointment. This meant that in my first season we flirted with relegation, which was far too close for comfort for me.

I was optimistic going into my second season when I brought in a few more players to strengthen the squad. I was convinced they could elevate the club. We were mid-table by the turn of the year but, more worryingly, we looked like a side that would not challenge for promotion, and would always struggle to keep in touch with the play-off places.

On top of that, there was an incident at a club function when, having over-indulged at the bar, I insulted a local butcher who happened to be a major sponsor of Peterhead. It wasn't remotely clever of me as this man, Kevin, who was also drunk, bore the brunt of a series of insults after we engaged in an argument. My barbed comments included me describing his meat – he used to give us free goody-bags of steaks and other products from his shop – as 'shite'. It was juvenile behaviour and embarrassing, though my only lapse at Peterhead.

I apologised to Kevin whose meat, despite my insults, was first class and who had been extremely kind and generous to me during my time at the club.

My spell with the Blue Toon side, though, was far from disastrous. At the same time, I didn't set the heather on fire and it would be fair to say they never got the best out of me. The financial situation at the club wasn't great, partly because I had taken in some players who were too expensive and not good enough to be challenging for the championship. However, it must be said that there were clubs like Ross County, Airdrie

United and Raith Rovers who were in our league and operating with full-time players.

In the end, it was my responsibility and while I didn't see my sacking coming – we were fifth in the league – I think Rodger had sussed that I wasn't focused on the job and that it was best to move me on. I simply wasn't justifying my wages and my demise was my own fault.

When the axe fell, the chairman had requested a private word after he, Neale and I had had a chat about matters in general.

'I have bad news for you,' he said. 'I've decided to call it a day with you.' Our manager–chairman relationship had been reasonable but I think he recognised that he didn't get the Steve Paterson he thought he'd hired and that I wasn't functioning too well.

It was an amicable parting and I left with three months' salary as I had never signed a contract, even though when I agreed to take the job, he asked me if I wanted a three or four-year deal. Call it naïve, or unworldly, or sheer stupidity, but I omitted to take advantage of the contract. At the parting of the ways I was just happy with what I was given to stave off some of my creditors.

The chairman told me he intended asking Neale to carry on and I endorsed his thinking. After all, Neale was doing a good job and there was no reason why he should be sacked as Duncan and Oshor had been at Aberdeen. I immediately told Neale what had happened and that he had my blessing to assume command, but I felt a certain sense of pride when I learned that Dave McGinlay had rejected Rodger Morrison's invitation for him to become Neale's assistant. Dave told me he didn't want to be there if I wasn't.

So ended a brief and disappointing spell. It was another rejection by me of a great chance – I had cocked a snook once more at the latest in a catalogue of lifelines.

I was sacked for only the second time in my managerial career and I was shocked. My life was careering out of control and I proved incapable of snapping myself out of the deep rut in which I was stuck.

All I could do was reaffirm my dalliance with William Hill or Corals or Scotscoup.

A holiday in the sun . . . almost

I felt a sense of relief to be sacked by Peterhead. I was not motivated by the job and had never felt fully engaged. As usual, I was heavily in debt and my money was continuing to go only one way.

I had a few months of moping about and I knew further football opportunities would be limited given that, after 15 successful years in management, I had now been sacked twice in quick succession, latterly by a club from a lower division. Club chairmen were hardly going to be banging down my door with job offers.

I needed a bit of self-analysis and to address the more important and pressing issues in my life. I was down, but not as low as I had been after being bulleted by Aberdeen.

It was time to re-enter social work and in April 2008 I took a job in a residential school near Banff. I needed to work to bring in some money but I was not interested in trying to get back into football at any level. A break from football was what I required and the game probably needed a break from me.

With Terri having tired of my disruptive behaviour and unpredictable lifestyle, she decided to cut me loose in April 2008, and my spirits plummeted. Nevertheless, I found my social work job more fulfilling and I worked hard for four months of long hours. What better way, then, to re-charge the batteries by taking Jessica and Emily on a two-week summer sunshine break abroad?

I decided that, as soon as I received my pay-cheque at the end of July, I would head, not to the bookies, but to a travel agent to book us a holiday. I had been doing well at work and had cut down dramatically on my drinking, although the betting shops were still a huge attraction.

I was putting in 50-hour weeks and felt good about myself, particularly as I was about to give my daughters a deserved vacation.

Having £2,000 of wages at my disposal, however, brought the usual thoughts. Surely, the sensible thing to do would be to double it on the horses. After all, I was never going to lose. Was I?

I set off for Keith and rapidly it was all gone, bar £90. That was all I had left. What would I tell my daughters? How would they cope with another disappointment, especially as they were looking forward so much to hitting the beaches of Tenerife? I had just chucked away almost £2,000. Almost.

There was only one option – to use what I had left to recoup my losses and, with a little help from up above, do even better. The £90 was placed on bets in two bookies – in Keith and in Elgin – and at the end of the day I was richer by £6,000. Thank God. Now, I would be able to return home to inform Jessica and Emily not that I had almost come a cropper with the holiday fund, but that everything was in hand and that they could look forward to having a great time. After all, I had three times more money to spend than I'd had earlier that day. I was ecstatic.

Then it came to me: if I could conjure up £6,000 from £90, what could I produce out of the hat with the larger sum? The following day, I could hardly wait for the bookies to open. By the time they had closed several hours later, they had it all, every penny of that £6,000. My plans and those of my daughters crumbled thanks to a selfish father whose only thoughts were for his own need to gamble.

I did not feel good about myself. I was now on leave from my job with no money and a bucketful of self-loathing. My recklessness coincided with Speyfest, an annual music festival in Fochabers which attracts many thousands of people, most with a capacity for consuming gallons of alcohol. Would I like a job serving drinks in the beer tent? Such an offer was music to my ears. At the end of each night me and anybody else who cared – and there were many – partied into the wee small hours.

Being broke put me into a negative mode of heavy drinking. I think that was the moment when I gave up. It was my rock bottom, my all-time low. I was defeated. I drank every day in August, borrowing money from anybody who would give me it – my mother, friends, people in bars. I felt like a low-life and my behaviour became even more insane and inconceivable.

I had been working up to 200 hours a month then doing what I did best, blowing it at the bookies. Frankly, it was getting me down. There I was, 34 years after I first dipped my toe in the shark-infested waters of gambling, and I was still behaving as I had when I was 17, having tossed away £1m-plus – a very conservative estimate – in the intervening years.

It is soul-destroying. You work hard for your money, you have bills to pay, but you give everything you've earned to a bookmaker – the same old cycle. Sure, I would have wins, perhaps £4,000 or £5,000, but they would soon disappear along with my earnings.

I was 50 and out of football and I felt washed-up. What a mess I had made of my life. And what a mess I was still making. I was unable to conquer my demons and I felt deep in a rut.

That summer, my rent arrears had grown and I lapsed on other bills. By then I had entered a trust deed agreement, a legal process which is a last step before bankruptcy where your debt is written off and you pay an agreed figure over three years. My debts to credit card companies and banks exceeded £100,000 and it was agreed that I would pay a certain amount of money in the pound.

Sure, I admit to having wallowed in self-pity, but it was worse than that because I sought comfort in alcohol. Despite that, I was always ready to work, even though it was only to feed my gambling habit.

In May 2009, a mate of mine who runs a pub in Fochabers as well as providing security for various agricultural shows, offered me work on a weekend off from my full-time job. I had just gambled away my April salary so the thought of picking up £300 for three days' effort, was appealing.

'We're going to Ayr Agricultural Show,' he said, 'and your job will be to look after the car park.'

The event was staged at the famous Ayr racecourse and a clutch of us were bussed from Fochabers to the south-west of Scotland and put up in a budget hotel for the duration. On the first day I was handed a walkie-talkie and a luminous jacket and sent to my post.

'Look who it is,' one of the show organiser's said, smiling as he walked towards me. 'The finest footballer ever to come out of the Highlands. What the fuck are you doing here?'

I have never had an ego that would prompt embarrassment in such situations. I always took the view that I am just like any other working person, except that I had been fortunate to have had several high profile and lucrative jobs. But whether it was managing a Premier League team or ushering vehicles into a car park, it didn't matter. It was just another job.

The Ayr Show is large-scale with thousands of visitors over the weekend and, inevitably, others were to recognise me.

'Hey, were you no' the Aberdeen manager?'

'Hoh . . . it's that guy who got the bullet fae Aberdeen. He's come down in the world, eh? Working as a fuckin' car park attendant.'

Those epitomised the general tone of the comments. They did not worry me. I would smile and say something equally empty back. Strangely, I enjoyed that gig, ensuring that cars were lined up properly and that everything was in order. It certainly was a far cry from leading Caley Thistle to that famous win over Celtic or some of the encounters I had at grounds like Pittodrie or Ibrox.

I have no false pride or a belief that I'm somebody special. If I had to dig ditches I would. Maybe that was part of my problem when I was the Aberdeen manager. I had never truly felt worthy of the job. I'm an ordinary guy who perhaps lacked confidence.

36

Taking the big step

Back in 2005, post-Aberdeen, when I had gone through one of my many mad periods of drinking and gambling, Oshor gave me the telephone number of the Sporting Chance Clinic. You couldn't be referred. You had to be the one to make contact, proving that you were serious by taking that first step to conquering your addiction.

In my deep moments of remorse I told myself I needed to try the clinic. I needed a chance. I had been to my GP and was offered counselling and I was on anti-depressants which only took the edge off how low I felt. They were not the answer.

I was signed off work. I simply couldn't face it. I was a mess. The wounds I had inflicted on myself were now bringing me to heel. My only relief was either being drunk or asleep and I found it impossible to function. I lay in bed for hours in my depression, usually staring at the ceiling or trying to force my brain to wipe everything out.

Could I sort my life and find myself once more? Too many people cared for me. Four years after Oshor had sourced that phone number it was time to make the call.

I was apprehensive, scared almost, to pluck up the courage to call the clinic, but I did and was disappointed when I was put on to voicemail.

I mumbled a message that I wanted to speak to someone about the possibility of entering the clinic and the following day, Peter Kay, Sporting Chance's chief executive, telephoned me and engaged me in a lengthy conversation. I found him re-assuring and understanding. He told me I would have to go through an assessment but, based on what I told him, he felt I was a worthy recipient of their programme of treatment. I was relieved that I had finally surrendered and admitted defeat.

That call was important to get the wheels in motion and at the end of August 2009, a week or two after my call to Peter, I travelled down to meet James West, one of the clinic's main therapists. Despite having spoken to Peter on the telephone, I was still drinking heavily every single day, hoping to blot out my misery.

I flew from Inverness to Southampton and spent the night at Champneys. Jessica came with me and she literally held my hand all the way as I was in a zombie-like state. My assessment lasted two hours, during which time I poured out my story and at the end of it I was told that the scale of my problems indicated that I was clearly a candidate needing help. There followed an agonising wait, four weeks in total, for the next in-take of clients. It was a troubled month after I received the official letter giving me my entry date. I was desperate for aid, yet I found myself in this limbo as I looked ahead to entering this unusual pact and giving myself over to the experts. I just wanted help, instantly.

My world had fractured to such a degree that I didn't care what happened to me.

On a couple of weekends I ended up in Keith with people I didn't really know but who wanted to be able to tell their pals they'd been drinking with Pele. I would meet them in pubs, sometimes fall asleep in bars and finish my binges in the homes of strangers on Saturday nights then waken up and head straight to a pub as soon as it was opening time on Sunday mornings. I remember walking the eight miles home from Keith one Sunday afternoon, penniless and pathetic.

It was a sad state of affairs, particularly for my daughters, who could only look on at a father who was a crumbling, drunken wreck, always self-centred and incapable of accepting responsibility.

I thought I was such a liability that it would be better all round

– certainly for those I had let down – if I wasn't there, if I ended my life. Could this be the only way out of my hell?

I had been given the lifeline of the Sporting Chance and it is no exaggeration to state that had I not had that, by Christmas I would have been in the gutter, or in a psychiatric unit, or dead.

I may have slipped here and there in my gambling but there is no doubt the clinic has had a dramatic and positive impact on my life and given me an awareness and an insight into my problems, my addictions and an understanding that what I have is an illness.

You can be helped but you have to be proactive to win your battle. It can be won, as Tony Adams, who founded Sporting Chance, has shown.

It helped me appreciate my family and my friends. It helped me in the writing of this book and reminded me that, beyond the horrors of my gambling and drinking and the debris I left everywhere, I had to recognise that I'd had a privileged life. Football had been good to me, not just financially, but in life experiences and afforded me the opportunity to meet some fascinating people. My life had many plus-points and I was lucky to have such a supportive family and friends.

There are addicts of my age who are down and outs or living in hostels and who have lost their marriages, their children and their friends. There but for the grace of God go I. Where would I be had my folks abandoned me?

It is a nightmare when you are being harassed by debt agencies and you are about to be evicted. My mother, Jon and Nige and Mick, have all written out cheques for thousands of pounds to stop me from going under.

I was always prepared to work, however, and will continue to work to my dying day. Indeed, after being discharged from Forest Mere, I got straight back to my job in a residential home, an occupation which has made me realise that, despite my troubles, there are people – notably the children with whom I work – worse off by far.

37

The social worker with a Guinness and a bookie's pen

I started out on the social work path in Elgin in 1987 and worked in residential homes for a decade before becoming a full-time football manager with Inverness Caley. Many years then passed as boss of that team before the other full-time roles came along at Aberdeen and then at Peterhead, though intermittently, social work has been my 'real' job with its main thread being looking after adolescents in the 12–16 years age group, kids who have social, emotional, family and many other difficulties. It is a profession that is both challenging and demanding but one that also has its rewards.

I could never have been a salesman or anything to do with technical work. I'm a people person and I think my man-management was one of my strengths in football. But I look at children in the care system and feel sad for them because, through circumstances, they've had a raw deal from life.

Despite my troubles, my daughters have never wanted for anything. I don't believe I have done them long-term psychological damage. The children I have encountered in my professional role, however, can't count themselves so fortunate.

It's a tough job. I work with a lot of anger in young folk and that can be projected on to you. I've been assaulted, spat on and called all the names under the sun but I have never taken those incidents personally. Those kids have a great deal of angst and fury in them and sometimes I have simply got in the way of that.

Today, I meet boys and girls who came through the system

and now have their own families and who have done well in life, and that is heartening to see. They have broken the cycle and they have been a success. It makes me feel proud that what I do is meaningful and helpful to those young, vulnerable and disadvantaged people with whom I come into contact.

There is, however, also a down side, and that manifests itself in the kids who have taken drug overdoses or others who have ended up in prison. It is tragic.

Many people take for granted the life they have with parents, aunties and uncles and other members of extended family. On the other hand, there are too many children who have been abandoned at a young age, have never known their parents or their families, who then enter the care system, leave it at 16 or older, and go into B&B accommodation with nobody else in the world. In a perfect society no child should be in care.

My time in the clinic was well publicised and I have had adverse comments about that. I remember taking a job after leaving Aberdeen FC and all the bad publicity that went with it, and there were other social workers who expressed concern that I was back working in residential care. I did not take offence as it was a perfectly reasonable point, though I admit to some hurt over it.

I have always been open: my problems would never impinge on my work in childcare and my employers have certainly been supportive and understanding.

When I was taking my social work diploma at the time I was managing Huntly, some of the players would joke: 'Some social worker you are, a Guinness in one hand and a bookie's pen in the other.'

For many who know the erratic nature of my life, I guess the last type of work I would be expected to undertake would be social work, but those employed in the care system with whom I have come in contact are genuine, dedicated and caring. At the old Andrew Thomson House where I started there were two great ladies who served a large number of kids in Moray over the years.

'Granny Wibbs' and 'Annie Mack' had no formal social work qualifications but provided old-fashioned motherly love to the youngsters in their care. Of course, the profession has come in for a battering from time to time because of abuse committed by people trusted to look after vulnerable and often neglected and psychologically flawed kids.

Thankfully, with new stringent methods of vetoing and examining workers with police and other checks, abuse should be a thing of the past. Nevertheless, this will be of little comfort to those who have been the victims of the abusers and paedophiles who slipped through the net. They ruined a great many lives and many victims sought solace in alcohol and drugs while others were led to suicide as the only way to end their pain.

Recently, I met a lad in a shop who I had in care for four years in Forres. He was one of those likeable rogues who had come from a poverty-stricken childhood in which he had been neglected. Unfortunately, he had fallen into the trap of drugs and crime.

He used to come to Caley's games and training sessions and the lads had adopted him as a kind of mascot but, despite such preferential treatment, he couldn't resist stealing from the dressing room while we were working out. I had had no option but to ban him.

That day when our paths crossed again he was pleased to see me and acted like he'd just been re-acquainted with a long-lost relative. We even swapped mobile phone numbers. When we were in the shop I asked him what he had been doing with himself.

'Oh, I've just dropped off some dope,' he replied. 'I'm working for a dealer in Aberdeen.' Then he added: 'I've just scammed the shop of £50 from scratch cards.'

'I never heard that,' I told him.

So, not much, if anything, had changed in the ten or more years since those days I took him to Caley. However, he was an exception, in my experience. And I am proud of all the young folk who have made a success of their lives post-care.

Since leaving Peterhead and recognising the extent of my own problems and how they needed to be confronted, my return to social work at a residential school provided me with a feeling that I was doing something meaningful. I just wish our government would do more to help support those who have come through the care system through to young adulthood.

Social work is a far from lucrative job at my end of the scale and because of my gambling excesses I will never be able to afford retirement. Maybe between social work and football I'll get by.

My annual pension statement came in from Moray Council which informed me that, at the age of 65, I'll receive a lump sum of £3,000 and a weekly allowance of £30.

Funny, when I was a heavy punter I would have regarded that £3,000 as handy for a good week at Cheltenham. The £30 would have bought me six pints of Guinness twice a week. Some retirement.

Undeserved support

'It's Pele. I need your help.' How often I have uttered those words to family and friends over my life. Jon Law, my close pal who moved from Moray to Manchester, Mick Connolly and Nigel Smith, other good mates, have heard those six words far too frequently for the liking of their bank managers.

They have bailed me out time and again, as has Oshor Williams, a Christian man who has turned the other cheek more times than I care to remember. They have listened to my hard-luck tales of woe and financial difficulties and come to my aid at each time of asking.

And then there is the unstinting, unwavering love of my mother, a gem of a woman who has not deserved the misery and heartache this feeble human being has brought her. How have I repaid her? With lies and deceit, and the theft of so much money that it makes me weep to think how many times I have betrayed her.

When she would give me her debit card to allow me to take out £50 I would invariably end up taking more from her account. She forgave me. When I removed cash from her home, convincing myself I would have winnings to allow me to replace the 'loan' before she returned and still have a profit, it was always the bookies who would benefit. She forgave me.

Indeed, she never saw any return on her involuntary invest-ments and I'm ashamed of myself for doing that to a woman who would give me every drop of blood in her body. Her financial assistance and that of others, including my daughters, got me out of many a hole with sheriff's officers and court officials, but it never addressed the underlying problems. I had to stop asking because I knew I couldn't be trusted.

I can see how people who embezzle money, particularly for gambling, find themselves in such a fix. I fully understand why some take their own lives. God knows, I've flirted with such thoughts.

My mother had breast cancer a few years back and suffered, too, from diabetes. She had a hard life and worked when she was young in the canteen of Mosstodloch Primary School. She is well-known in the area as Mrs P and is popular and respected in the community. She is a caring and gentle person with a soft centre. Karen, my girlfriend of 20 years ago, and Mandy, my ex-wife, still visit her and some of my mates will call into her flat in Fochabers.

She would take her daily walk to the shop or the Post Office in Mosstodloch and it would take her two hours before she returned because so many people would stop her and talk. I see her most days and so do my sister and my niece. She has good family support.

She has been the lynchpin of the Paterson brood. My dad was a hard-working man and, in many ways, a lonely figure, while my mum was the centrepiece of the household and there for all her family.

My mother loves football and enjoyed my involvement in the game and often came to watch me. She is teetotal but used to like a little flutter, which would sometimes allow her to stop thinking of the worry and misery I have caused her, particularly in the last decade. She demanded to know where my problems lay and she took on a lot of the burden of my gambling and drinking.

Even to this day she would tell me she didn't mind me having a bet as long as I treated it as a bit of fun. If only that were possible. Her message was straightforward: everything in moderation. Sadly, her advice was never heeded.

She helped me enormously and bailed me out of more financial trouble than anybody by handing me money to settle bills I simply could not pay. She did it out of love for me but her generosity did not help and merely fuelled my habit. She hated to see me unhappy and troubled.

When she would find out that I had taken her debit card and helped myself to her savings in order to gamble, and then lose her money, she always extended the open arms of love, despite her exasperation and upset. I loathe myself for the way I behaved towards her. I hate having to face up to the fact that I stole from the woman who has loved me all of my life. Those and other aspects of my relationship with her do not rest easy with me and my guilt on that score still rankles. Do I feel a scumbag? Oh yes. And that feeling will never go away. I don't see myself as a thief but my addiction has caused me to be one and commit other misdemeanours which, in all honesty, horrify me.

My mum has had her fair share of sadness with the loss of loved ones and I think the very least she could have expected was to have lived the later stages of her life with the kind of peace of mind and contentment she clearly did not get because of me. I do go out of my way to care for her and support her. But I have loaded her with too many burdens. She has taken them on her shoulders and tried to help me. She has been dejected and in tears on so many occasions, pleading with me to give up my destructive ways.

My problems were so deep, so ingrained, that I would not, could not, turn my back on them. They owned me. Every single time I have asked, she has stepped in to help me, giving me money which would never be paid back, I would pledge to change my ways and, at least for a period, I would try hard to turn my back on gambling and drinking.

It was never to last, of course, and I would be back to where I was, betting too much, seeking the numbing effect of booze and sitting down with my mother to beg for more money. She never said no. What a pathetic state of affairs for a grown man with an elderly mother.

I do have a conscience and the strain and stresses and worry I heaped on her over a long, long period will live with me till the day I die. To this day those thoughts drive me towards moods which are as low as I get.

I know I gave her joy, though, when I was a young player and then when I became a successful manager. I think I made her proud of me, if only for a time. The darker side which went along with my success was always there and she knew it. She lived with it every bit as much as I did.

Thankfully, her love has never gone away. The feeling is reciprocated and I know how fortunate I am to have had a mother who is nothing short of special.

As many of the stories in this book have highlighted, there is an immaturity about me that reinforced my failure to grow up emotionally, still behaving like a 20-year-old even though I was a middle-aged man. I wanted life's better things without having to put in any great effort.

I was a gifted young football player and blessed with natural assets as a manager but my addictions held me back and would not allow me to develop my talents. Perhaps subconsciously I avoided responsibility by gambling, whether it was placing a bet on the 2.30 at Newmarket, or stacking £100 chips on the roulette wheel, or accepting a card at blackjack.

I also had this inner urge to be a 'big shot' and the centre of attention by relaying my stories of my gambling exploits. I was desperate to maintain a 'Pele the lad' image that I thought would impress others.

There is a theory that compulsive gamblers subconsciously want to lose in order to punish themselves and I have to admit to having carried a large element of self-destruct behaviour around with me for years into many areas of my life, particularly in relationships and my career.

I have had five serious and loving relationships with women, each of which has been sabotaged by my gambling and drinking. These women were special and committed and loving, but I drove them away. I deeply regret that, especially with my last relationship – with Terri – which ended in 2008 after almost six years.

Why am I incapable of retaining the love of women who have been willing to believe in me, to help and support me? I wish I had an answer. The inability to accept reality and emotional insecurity have undoubtedly played their part in my addiction.

I believe in the Gamblers Anonymous and Alcoholics Anonymous fellowships and their ethos of accepting spiritual values and qualities like generosity, honesty, tolerance and humility – all principles they advocate as a way of life. Such spiritual fellowships should not be misinterpreted as some kind of religious society.

People from all walks of life and denominations are welcomed, as are atheists and agnostics. Unity and, of course, anonymity are key in those organisations and anyone with a desire to stop gambling, drinking, or using drugs could do worse than seek their help.

If nothing else comes out of this book, I hope there is at least a warning to young people, not just those in the football world, that if they have a problem with any kind of addiction, they should seek help sooner rather than later.

Each day they ignore their addiction, or refuse to acknowledge that they are in the control of one, is a crucial day lost in their precious lives. They must remember that help is available and they should embrace it with enthusiasm.

I hope there may be youngsters who will read this account of wasted time and lost opportunities and feel that if they are losing their way through drink, drugs or gambling, they can become aware that help is at hand. All they need to do is ask.

39

'A huge loss to the game'

I was heartened by the level of support, much of it from people I didn't even know, for my decision to seek help from the Sporting Chance Clinic. Of course, it wasn't until I returned home after my four-week stay there that I was made aware of the feelings of others over my addictions.

Reading through the various newspaper reports of how people inside and outside football reacted, gave me a lift and kept me going for a time, underlining how right I had been to seek the help on which I had previously turned my back.

Duncan Shearer, my loyal assistant at Aberdeen, was quoted as saying he had been aware of my problems, although he admitted he had not known the scale of my gambling addiction.

'We got the occasional glimpse that Steve was maybe betting a bit more than average,' he told *Aberdeen Evening Express* sportswriter, Charlie Allan. 'But I had no idea he was gambling to the extent he has now admitted to. The first I knew things were really bad was when Oshor Williams called to say he was trying to persuade Steve to go in for treatment. I'm pleased Steve has now taken Oshor's advice and checked into the clinic down in England. My main hope now is that he can eventually get back to the stage where he can enjoy his life again.'

Duncan was good enough also to praise my ability as a coach, citing that I had a 'marvellous football brain' and that it was sad that 'a man as talented as Steve has slipped out of the game'.

I appreciated those compliments but there was one comment

that hit home. It centred on what happened during what was supposed to be our great adventure at Aberdeen.

'We hardly kept in touch after that,' he said. 'I reckon it was because Steve was a little embarrassed by how things went at Aberdeen. He probably felt he had let me down because it meant my time at Pittodrie was up as well. He had no need to feel like that because I have no regrets.'

I can't overstate how reassuring it was to read those sentiments, especially as Duncan was right to assume that I was, indeed, dreadfully ashamed and embarrassed over how my crazy behaviour had impacted so powerfully on him and Oshor and their families. Such magnanimity is undeserved.

Alex Smith, a former Aberdeen manager who held similar posts at Dundee United and Ross County, was another who offered words of comfort and encouragement. In his column in the *Press & Journal* newspaper on 3 October 2008, three days after my admission to Sporting Chance, he wrote that my decision to check in to the clinic was brave and one that should be applauded.

'Gambling, and to a lesser extent drinking, go hand in hand with football,' he commented. 'A player can be goaded by his team-mate into trying to outdo him and before you know it, they are hooked. I have only had to intervene once as a manager and that was on a very small scale. The younger players who had joined the first-team squad were playing cards with the senior players and betting way beyond their means. As the senior pros betted within their means, the youth players were being enticed into horrendous financial problems and I quickly nipped it in the bud.'

How I wish Alex had been around in my days as a young player, though I fear he may have found me a lost cause. Still, I was grateful for his clear support in his newspaper column as he expressed a genuine hope that I would survive my personal demons.

'Steve's two daughters and his mother will be his motivation,' he wrote, 'and I would imagine his plea for help has come as a huge relief to everyone who knows him. Steve is one of the game's good guys and I hope he can come through his problems and make a return to football one day. He has other issues more important than football right now, but it would be a huge loss to the game if a mentally fit and capable Steve Paterson was not involved at some level.'

Given Alex Smith's standing in the game, his remarks and observations helped me during those difficult days of post-clinic rehabilitation.

In my bad moments, however – those horrible days when I have lapsed and headed for a betting shop – I am filled with shame that he is just one of a long line of people I have let down.

40

A relapse confession on the path to a better life

I left the Sporting Chance Clinic on 26 October 2009, after 28 days of rehab. I felt like a new man, full of energy and spark. It was the best I had felt, physically and mentally, for more than 20 years. I guess you could equate it with being freed from prison after a long, long sentence for a crime you hadn't committed.

The first week on the 'outside' was spent in Manchester, where I stayed with Jon Law, his wife Jen and their daughter, Harriet. What would I have done throughout my disaster of a life without people like them?

I admire Jon, my former school friend from Fochabers, not only for his professional achievements in teaching but also for his strength in dealing with the loss of his beloved son, Jamie, at the tender age of 21 in 2003. Jon's loss and sadness and the dignified manner in which he coped, made me feel embarrassed that I considered my difficulties such a big deal.

Jon had left Milne's High School with a couple of Standard Grades and went to Manchester with another of my other pals, Ainslie Gordon. That was in 1976, a year after I joined Manchester United. Jon's determination to do well saw him blag his way into teacher training college where he worked hard for his degree in education and his tough and dogged approach to his work saw him rise through the ranks to become a head teacher, a job that, he admits, brought him some interesting experiences, including seeing guns – real ones - in the playground.

Jon and I still have a great deal in common, other than drinking and gambling, which he controls and manages in a sensible manner. Generally, our outlook on life has always been similar.

My post-rehab week with Jon, Oshor, Mick Shaw, Mick Connolly and Nige Smith, was extremely enjoyable. Those pals have been a source of great support, more especially in the past seven years. I owe them a great deal . . . and not just cash. I try to spend time with them three or four times a year and I enjoy every single minute of it.

My return to Fochabers following my stay in the clinic was heart-warming, being reunited with my darling girls, going for a meal and catching up with all the news. They were genuinely proud and pleased to see and hear their dad looking and sounding so well.

I took the decision to immerse myself in work and activity, ensuring I filled the void previously reserved for my ruinous activities. I re-started my job, putting in up to 50 hours a week at the residential home where I work in the north of Scotland.

Life was tough but it was good. And then came the blip, the moment I had dreaded. The episode I knew was always just round the corner, even though it seemed to be on some kind of slow burn.

Six men sat round a table in a room in Inverness. 'My name's Steve and I am a gambling addict.' I looked across at the two young men opposite and as I laid bare my rubbish dump of a life as a gambler and serial boozer, my mind contained thoughts that those youngsters facing me were at the beginning of their road to hell. If only I could help them. Christ, if they can nip it now, they're young enough to start again. Surely, they will hear my story and say: 'Bugger that. We're not going to end up like that bum.'

Gamblers Anonymous doesn't attract huge numbers to meetings in the Highland capital. Maybe my experience of the one or two occasions I attended simply failed to inspire me. The whole affair seemed listless. Or was it just me? Did I really have my heart in this?

There must be more people in this town, I thought, who are addicted to betting in all its guises: on-line, sports, or horse racing, even one-arm bandits. Keep going to the meetings, the books tell you. It's what the therapists at the clinic told me. Where was everybody?

When I graduated from Sporting Chance I had felt re-energised. For the first few months, whether it was a knock-on, feel-good thing or whatever, I felt better than I had done for years. I went to a few AA meetings but rarely to GA gatherings because their Aberdeen meeting was on a Saturday at two o'clock and at Inverness on a Sunday at lunchtime, where attendances were sparse. I should have made more of an effort, at least for Inverness. Unwisely, I didn't. I had managed to get through without drinking and gambling for several months but I found that, on weekends off, I hadn't filled the void.

Watching Jeff Stelling present Sky's Gillette Soccer Saturday was too much to bear. I had allowed my visits to the gym to slip. Neither could I concentrate on reading a book. Sooner than I believed could happen, my defences were under attack. I cracked, and my desire to have a bet, my first for several months, was just too much to resist.

Just a £20 or £30 treble, I thought. That could do no harm, surely. How foolish and weak. How self-indulgent. The slow, subtle, insidious path towards relapse was forming in my head.

I may have resisted entering the betting shop in Keith first time round, despite driving there and sitting outside in my car, but it was mental torture. That shop, Scotscoup, must have taken around £250,000 off me over the years but as I sat in the beat-up old banger of a VW Polo I had at the time, smoked a couple of fags over a 20-minute period, I fought off the demons who were pressing me to place my bet. It was a close shave and one I should have heeded. Why hadn't I simply phoned Osh or Donald or Jon? No, I kept it inside my own head.

That abortive trip to the bookies where the voice which demanded that I drive away from that betting shop was louder than the one telling me there was no harm in going in, sticking a bet on and enjoying myself, was at the end of January 2009.

But the craving, the burning need to have a bet, just one solitary punt, ate away at me throughout the following month. Then circumstances conspired to gang up on me; Friday, 27 February, pay day, a day off – a combination destined to lead to disaster as months of abstinence, no betting and certainly no thought of taking a drink, were wiped away in one winter's afternoon. Five bets accompanied by frenzy. OK, I won a few hundred quid but with my winnings came guilt, feelings of weakness and failure. I regarded myself a cheat and toe-rag.

My recovery was jeopardised and my gambling quickly accelerated and carried on through March and most of April; horses, dogs, football, golf and, as the saddest of the sad punters in that betting shop, on the video roulette wheel.

If that wasn't bad enough I even betted on the 'cartoon' races to fill in a five-minute lull in my gamblefest madness. Those are virtual races, an insult to anyone's intelligence and, in my view, out of order for bookmakers to promote. But then, they must rely on people like me, the weak and the foolish among their clientele.

I had lost control and could see my life moving unmanageably towards a cliff edge. It wasn't as if I hadn't been warned by those at the clinic that one little bet would lead to the old chronic ways. Peter Kay, James West, Julian Keeling and Chris Mordue, my dedicated and highly skilled and knowledgeable therapists at Sporting Chance, were right. My wheels had come off.

On 1 May 2009, the day before Jessica's twenty-first birthday party, a feeling of misery and hopelessness enveloped me. My losses meant – again – that I had no means with which to cover my outgoings. These were my thoughts that night:

GA tells you not to carry much money. I shouldn't have access to money. That's how pathetic it is. I want to give up. I don't want to go to work. I don't want to see anybody. I wish I could be locked up for a year or two, away from money, responsibility and temptation. That's how I feel. That would cure me. It would also punish me, something I deserve, for all the lies and stealing from my own folk and for not paying them back what I owe them.

Imagine, if I went out and robbed someone in the street, I would rightly end up behind bars. Yet, in effect, that's what I'm doing to people who love me and who have supported me every inch of the way.

The worst part for me is the depression. I don't see any point in living, despite the many things I've got going for me: my daughters and my mother, and my friends. I have a job and I have achieved a great deal in my football career but it's all totally irrelevant because of gambling.

I need to get a fucking grip. I'm staring once more into the dark abyss and the demons are calling my name. Tomorrow is Jessica's twenty-first birthday bash and I am hiding in my room. I must summon the courage to get me back on track, otherwise my recovery is history. All the hard work in the clinic and since coming out will be destroyed. The only way forward for me is the Gamblers Anonymous programme.

That self-examination, my DIY analysis, changed my thinking and tore me away from my addiction. Was it because I felt more hellish than I had done before? Or was it that magic moment when something just clicked in my brain, telling me that I was too old for all of this? Why should I continue to adversely affect the lives of my loved ones?

I had spent three or four days in my room, in bed, not eating, not taking calls and not communicating. I was in a very bad place. My daughters tried to talk to me but I had neither the inclination nor the energy to answer.

It should have been a very happy time for Jessica in the days leading up to her party but she looked at her dad lying there feeling sorry for himself, wrapped up in his own world, co-cooned in his own selfish behaviour.

That May Day 2009 was a turning point. More than a hundred people, including my ex-wife Mandy, gathered in the village hall in Fochabers on the evening of 2 May to celebrate Jessica's big day. To think that only 24 hours earlier I had made up my mind that I could not possibly face anyone, never mind 100 partygoers. How could I? I had no money with which to contribute to the occasion and my mood was of gloom and despondency and self-loathing that a father could not play a meaningful part in such a significant moment in the life of his child.

Whatever little piece of character I had left in me, though, came to the fore and I made up my mind that I would not let Jessica down. It was as if there was a voice inside me saying: 'You *shall* go to the ball.'

It was a fancy dress party based on a 1980s theme, which meant I didn't have to try too hard to find appropriate clothing in my wardrobe. And so off I went, my shirt collar wrapped over the big lapels on my jacket and wearing flared trousers to join the merry band of revellers and looking like a poor man's John Travolta. I never knew you could have so much fun without drinking.

It was a wonderfully happy occasion, with Jessica taking centre stage and glad that her dad had been part of it. If it was at all possible, I was more pleased that I could share in her joy as I hoped she felt proud that I had not let her down.

I had climbed back on to my horse, so to speak, and admitted to myself that I needed help. Thankfully, I had the strength to seek it.

I owed it to my family, my friends, to the staff at the clinic and ultimately to myself. My relapse was not irretrievable, I believed, and I knew that if I took action and recognised where I had gone wrong I could rectify matters.

It was clear to me that were I to continue to gamble I would face more misery, more heartache, depression and despair, and, of course, a drain on my meagre finances. But a genuine, honest application to living in the manner recommended by GA promised happiness, self-respect and peace of mind, and despite the failures in my life, I recognised the burning embers that were there during my rehabilitation at Forest Mere. It was there that my bankrupt spirit had been reawakened and there that I was pointed in the direction of the more positive parts of my life.

Despite my flirtation once more with my bookmaker over that horrendous spell I thanked God for what he had given me. I was, I now came to accept, blessed.

I shook off the self-pity and told myself to stop thinking me, me, me all the time.

Hope reigns supreme

There is a higher level. I needed to cleanse myself of the lying and the cheating and the deceit and stop living in the past with guilt, remorse and regret. I made up my mind that I would be moving forward and not looking backwards. Who knows, maybe in time, through honesty and integrity, this tortured man will grow out of his stunted emotional development.

I vowed to make GA work for me and found the trips to Inverness for meetings comforting and symbolic, especially when I thought about the many times I had travelled that road from Fochabers as a different person in search of hedonistic pursuits. Now, I want something new and refreshing from the Highland capital.

God,
Grant me the serenity to accept the things I cannot change, the courage to change the things I can and the wisdom to know the difference.

That first, simple stanza of the Serenity Prayer, the cornerstone of Gamblers, Alcoholics and Narcotics Anonymous, is a powerful message for me.

More than anything else in this life, I am searching for peace of mind. I want to see my children happy, and my family and friends to know contentment that I am safe and out of harm. I do not want any more to be this troubled soul whose mind and body has been ravaged by gambling and drinking.

I consider myself lucky. I have seen the wrong side of life, even though it has taken me more than 30 years to accept that it was wrong. I don't know if I'll lapse and go back to drinking or gambling and wasting my life and squandering opportunities.

What I do know is that, particularly with gambling, it is the wrong path to tread and one that leads only to misery, disruption and unhappiness for me and others. My lapses have all concerned my gambling addiction but one day I hope I can be a responsible drinker who can enjoy the social aspect of visiting a pub with friends or family. In the meantime, gambling and drinking will be treated exactly the same. Abstinence is the only cure as I seek a peace I have never experienced in my adult life.

I would love my daughters to have the peace of mind they deserve, and I can give them that if I turn my back on the demons that have been in my life for such a long, long time. I will keep working on beating this terrible affliction.

I hope addicts who read this will come to realise there is help out there and that it is possible to piece your life back together. The GA, AA and NA programmes do work and addicts need to know that. The Sporting Chance Clinic drummed that into me and they were absolutely correct.

In my moments of clarity, which have become more and more frequent, I am positive there are better times ahead. I still possess the ability I displayed as a coach over 15 successive and highly successful years before joining Aberdeen, seasons that brought me trophies and titles, championships and cheers. That talent has not vanished. It's just that other aspects of my life got in the way.

I created exciting football teams that entertained supporters. I led those teams to achievements previously out of their grasp. That was no fluke.

My time may have passed for a return to league football management, but I firmly believe that my trials and tribulations, and the fact that I have come through them, have made me a better man, and most probably an improved team boss. Experience is, indeed, a great teacher.

Today, I have a crisper outlook than I have had for years and I am better equipped to shoulder responsibility. That, allied to my proven interpersonal skills, are what would make me the manager I could and should have been. One day, a football club prepared to give me one more chance, will discover that.

Despite my torture and troubles, there are still positives to be taken from my roller-coaster ride of a life. There were the heady days of Manchester United, my seven-and-a-half wonderful years at Caley Thistle and five thoroughly enjoyable ones at Huntly. Those times, where I was in my comfort zone, were my best.

I have a lovely family and great friends, and am now on an honest path. Whether I can keep to it remains to be seen. More than anything else there is love and faith in equal measure from my family and friends. There is also the hope I have for myself.

And it is comforting to know that, at least for some followers of the game who will remember my days as a player, I am still a Highland hero.

Index